"*The greatest truth I can share with humanity is that we have within us the very presence of God in what we call our soul.*" This quote from *BEYOND THE MYSTICAL NEAR-DEATH EXPERIENCE AND INTO THE UNITIVE EXPERIENCE* is one example of the great truths flowing throughout Nancy Clark's latest and *very* important book. Nancy eloquently describes what I have found in my study of over 4,000 near-death experiences: We are all one, including one with God. This book is a treasure trove of inspirational spiritual wisdom. You won't want to miss this exciting book! I enthusiastically recommend this exceptional book as essential to *everyone* interested in near-death experiences and spiritual enlightenment."

—Jeffrey Long, M.D., author of the New York Times bestselling *Evidence of the Afterlife: The Science of Near-Death Experiences*, and *God and the Afterlife: The Groundbreaking New Evidence for God and Near-Death Experience*

"Having had both a near-death experience and a unitive mystical experience – and having researched spiritually transformative experiences for nearly 40 years – Nancy Clark is in a unique position to share profound spiritual insights. This work is a generous, encouraging labor of love that will inspire readers to progress along the mystical path toward union with The Divine."

—Ross Kardwell, President Institute for Mystical Experience Research and Education

"Over the years, I've greatly enjoyed visiting with Nancy and reading her books. I consider her to be a highly evolved soul with a NDE and NDE-like induced 'street cred' who has much to share. Nancy is a perfect example of why Plato recommended that teachers and leaders come from the ranks of near-death experiencers. As you will learn, she perceived *being invited by the Light* to create this new book. All the above factors have contributed to a uniquely powerful and important book that I highly recommend."

—Mark Pitstick, MA, DC, SoulProof.com Greater Reality Living.com

"Over the last decade, Nancy and I have seemed to have spiritually bonded in how we see the world and the universe. In the process, I have discovered a friend with a clear, loving, honesty and clarity in her life purpose. She lives what she writes about. She walks her talk and what she believes in. Her newest addition to her collective "spiritual energy" is her best book yet. I have fervently read every book that she has written about in her book. This book presents a loving blueprint for the heart and spirit for seekers looking for the "light within" themselves. This book is GOLD for the soul!"

—Rev. Bill McDonald, author of *Alchemy of a Warrior's Heart,"*
Warrior: A Spiritual Odyssey and other books; International
Inspirational Speaker; & Founder of
The Spiritual Warriors Ministry

"Virtually all religions recognize the unity of all things and the universal longing of individuals to identify with and become one with the Creator who is pure Love. Nancy Clark describes this "unitive experience" and provides an essential and comprehensive guide to mystical encounters and the oneness of all that is. Drawing on the writings of mystics from many traditions, she helps us in our own journeys to enlightenment and growth that comes from the awareness of God's presence in our lives. Her personal experiences and spiritual journey remind us that the purpose of human existence is to learn from our own living and to become one with God who is pure love so that we may express that love to all others. This is a book that will help us to understand that we are a work in progress and in a continual state of becoming what God intends for us to be."

—Rev. Dr. Harry L. Serio, author of *The Dwelling Place of Wonder,*
Mysticism and Ministry

"I highly recommend Nancy Clark's newest book entitled *Beyond the Mystical Near-Death Experience and Into the Unitive Experience,* which explains how the fear of death should not hold power over us. Among other topics, she discusses Near-Death and Unitive Experiences of the saints, mystics and herself, and also the power of a Kundalini awakening. These direct experiences have people returning *knowing* God, which changes their consciousness and gives them new energy. There is now a willingness to investigate the invisible side of life, feeding our minds to grow and expand. Her last chapter discusses intuition- how it is improved over time with practice - and it trains people to rely more on emotional information that comes to their body and brain. This is the type of book one needs to rid themselves of the weeds of negativity while realizing that heaven and hell are within us depending on the thoughts we have and live by. It's an excellent read!"

—Rev. Karen E. Herrick, PhD, author of *Grandma, What Is a Soul?*

"I met Nancy Clark while working as a registered nurse, and became interested in NDEs. I was working at Children's Hospital in Columbus, OH and started asking children after their resuscitation if they had experienced any of the components of an NDE. They had some wonderful "seed" experiences as Nancy explains in this book.

Nancy does an excellent job of developing what the differences are between an NDE and a Unitive Experience. She experienced ONENESS with God, the Light etc. This experience is very rare. We are to live to make His "Kingdom come, His will be done on earth, as it is in heaven." We need to love everyone, including our enemies. That is very difficult to do- to forgive those that have hurt us.

Nancy's book is a must read for everyone in this broken world! My takeaway is to love others as God loves us!"

—Joyce Gibb, M.S., C.R.N.P

BEYOND
THE MYSTICAL
NEAR-DEATH EXPERIENCE
AND INTO THE UNITIVE
EXPERIENCE

NANCY CLARK

1st WORLD
PUBLISHING

Beyond the Mystical Near-Death Experience and Into the Unitive Experience

Nancy Clark

Copyright © 2018 Nancy Clark

Published by 1st World Publishing
P.O. Box 2211, Fairfi eld, Iowa 52556
tel: 641-209-5000 • fax: 866-440-5234
web: www.1stworldpublishing.com

First Edition
LCCN: 2018964845
Softcover ISBN: 978-1-4218-3818-2

This material has been written and published for educational purposes to enhance one's well-being. In regard to health issues, the information is not intended as a substitute for appropriate care and advice from health professionals, nor does it equate to the assumption of medical or any other form of liability on the part of the publisher or author. The publisher and author shall have neither liability nor responsibility to any person or entity with respect to loss, damages, or injury claimed to be caused directly or indirectly by any information in this book.

CONTENTS

DEDICATION

*To my Great Teacher, the One whose Love and Grace taught
me so much more about goodness and Light than I would
ever learn from this world in which I exist. May this book we
wrote together, inspire others to live in Your Peace, the true life
that only You can give.*

ACKNOWLEDGMENTS

"Tis only when they spring to Heaven that angels reveal themselves to you."

–Robert Browning

There have been angels right here on earth who have appeared to me during the writing of this book and I would like to thank them at this time.

Pat Stillisano, DDS; you held my hand throughout all my questions, all my brain-freezes, all my frustrations! How patient you were with me as I began learning about the mystics and saints, a subject I had no prior knowledge. How can I thank you for that? You are a genuine friend whose patience and encouragement has been a Divine gift.

Ken Ring, PhD; Professor Emeritus Psychology, University of Connecticut; internationally recognized authority on near-death experiences; Co-Founder of the International Association for Near-Death Studies (IANDS) and author of five books on the subject. Few people have the privilege of having such a supportive and giving friend. I am beyond lucky to have you in my life for so many years. Thank you for being here for me yet again. I am so grateful that you are my dear friend and mentor! I love you.

PMH Atwater; world noted near-death experience researcher and personal friend who understands the deep relationship between self and God after having had three near-death experiences herself. As an author of over 15 books, her research has contributed immensely to the NDE community. Thanks PMH for taking the time to know who I really am. You are a wonderful friend and I appreciate your love, kindness and support.

God works in mysterious ways, but it's no mystery to me that Mark Lutz is in my life. Bless you for your kindness and support. When I count my blessings I count you twice.

Columbus, Ohio International Association for Near-Death Studies, my heart and appreciation goes out to every member for believing in me and the work I am doing for the Light.

Without two of my computer friends who helped me when I couldn't solve problems on my own, they were there in a heartbeat to help me. Jeff Lutz and Rick Fisher, I am lucky to have you both.

William Hoover, M.D., I am enormously touched and appreciative that I can discuss the wisdom I learned from the Light without hesitation. I am deeply blessed.

Mark Pitstick, DC, Director of Education, Eternea; Director of The Soul Phone Project; author, *Greater Reality Living*, has been a dear friend for many years. Thank you Mark for your unwavering and cheerful support with all my many projects.

My dear Heavenly friend Vernon Sylvest, M.D. national recognized physician and author, *The Formula*, who left behind for me, the memory of a friendship that I will continue to cherish until we meet again on the other side. Vernon always saw the best in me and always encouraged my work for God. I know that he watched over me as I wrote this book, cheering me on. What a boundless treasure his friendship has given me.

Rodney Charles, my publisher at 1st World Publishing. We don't meet people by accident. They are meant to cross our path for a reason. If I could sit across the porch from God, I'd thank Him for all the help and support you have given me. I am incredibly fortunate to have a publisher like you. Thank you from the bottom of my heart for all you have done for me. I love you beyond measure!

My sons Chris and Randy, the Heavens opened up the day God blessed me to be your mother. Thank you for always seeing the best in me and for lifting me up when I need you.

My husband Ched, I know you are watching over me from Heaven, and each passing day brings me closer to you. One day I hope to hold your hand and walk with you again. Until then, I will keep thanking God every day for all the blessed years we were together. I love you!

NOTE

In writing this book, I realize that some people may not be comfortable with my use of the masculine pronouns with words like *he* or *his*. How we speak about God is often influenced by the traditional language of the church, the Bible, or writings of the mystics and saints. The masculine pronoun always crops up. For some people, the idea of relating to God can be difficult because of painful experiences, and they may want to resist the idea of God being a masculine entity. I did not personally experience God as either being masculine or feminine. I experienced God as divine *energy*.

Since God is beyond all concepts and form, and cannot be adequately described using language, I ask the reader's forgiveness in choosing to refer to God in the masculine pronoun. I suppose I am old-school and feel comfortable using those familiar terms. If you aren't comfortable when those masculine pronouns appear, then please substitute whatever word that you are more comfortable using. We're really all talking about the same Source after all.

INTRODUCTION

I had no plans on writing this book. Previously, I had written five books and I told myself that I was finished writing already. I felt that I had fulfilled my promise to God to communicate the messages I had received during ecstatic moments with the One who had gifted me, so it was time for me to now rest knowing I did my best to serve my Beloved and others.

Little did I know that on one cold winter's morning, my Beloved had a different plan for me. Something very magical happened that morning while drinking my coffee seated at the kitchen table. Looking out from the large patio window, there was something very beautiful about seeing the first rays of sunshine caress each newly fallen snow flake. Every snowflake that fell from Heaven was like an angel's kiss. It was a lovely moment of embracing the natural world with reverence in the woods where I live.

A herd of deer had passed in search of food buried under the many inches of snow. The tiny birds were swooping and vying to be the first at the birdfeeders. I took in all that beauty in all its nuance within this interlude of silence as I remained present in those moments of joy.

Suddenly, the words, *"Beyond the Mystical Near-Death Experience and Into the Unitive Experience"* jolted quickly into my mind. *What was that? Where did those words come from?* I wondered. I wasn't thinking of anything else at the time except the beauty of the freshly fallen snow.

Then, deep within me, there was a twinge of recognition that something more beautiful, something more precious had taken me to a place of divinity within me, catching my attention to write another book. My eyes flung wide open, lids slightly flapping in astonishment because up until that moment, I had no plans on writing another book. None! I had tasted the mystery and understood I was being taken into it.

What does the word unitive experience mean? I wondered. I soon began to realize my own inadequacy in writing about such a difficult subject. Although I didn't have an idea how to write about this subject, I didn't make excuses or try to get out of it even though it felt like an overwhelming project.

You see, it was during a spiritually transcendent experience I had in 1979, that I had a Sacred encounter with God. It was then that I was given the instruction by the Light-God to *"speak and write"* what my Great Teacher had revealed to me. I promised I would serve in this capacity until I drew my final breath. Each book I wrote was not my idea to write. Each book came from an inner awareness that my Beloved was stirring up the pot and letting me know it was time to write again. The "voice" I always heard within was my Beloved's Voice, given to me in what I can only describe as an intuitive, knowing feeling. Once I agreed to write a book, it became a partnership between my Source and me. I know that by myself, I cannot write. But with God sitting with me and inspiring my written words, only then, can I write. So it was pretty clear to me when I heard those words, *"Beyond the Mystical Near-Death Experience and Into the Unitive Experience"* that this was God letting me know it's time to write another book.

Despite feeling incompetent writing about the unitive experience which I knew nothing about, in the end, despite my hesitation, I wrote as I was told. But first I had to familiarize myself with the term "unitive experience." I had many transcendent experiences during my life including a near-death experience where I journeyed from death and woke up in the morgue. Another time, I had what is termed a near-death-like experience in which I had the same features of a classic near-death experience with the exception that I was not close to death, suffering serious illness or physical trauma. I also had many other psychic and mystical experiences throughout my lifetime. What I did not know however, until I embarked upon writing this book, is that my near-death-like experience is really the mystical *unitive experience.*

A dear friend of mine who spent many years studying the mystics and saints explained to me that while near-death experiencers went **to** the Light, in my case, during my so-called near-death-like experience, the Light came **to me with a calling.** Big difference! My friend was the one who taught me about unitive mystical experiences which apparently, are very, very rare.

I will get into that later in this book, but for now, it will suffice to say that during my mystical unitive experience, I had merged into oneness with God, having no sense of self. I learned that mysticism means *seeing* Oneness and unitive seeing means seeing *from* Oneness.

Oh my goodness, what is my Beloved asking of me this time? To write a book about the limited knowledge I have about mysticism and unitive experience seemed to be more than I was capable of grasping. Why does one do something so difficult that one would not ordinarily consider doing?

Why is my Beloved asking me to write this particular book? Why didn't my Beloved ask someone who was a religious scholar who could have easily written a book on this subject? Why me? Because I had *direct experiential knowledge* of the subject, not necessarily the scholarly knowledge, that's why, Nancy!

I must be honest, I never received any formal religious instruction growing up. I was only taught how to say my prayers and how to prepare for confession and Holy Communion. That's it! Also, I was never permitted to read the Bible because the priest warned the congregation that lay people can't understand the written word and only the priest could explain it to us. The problem for me was that I attended a Ukrainian Catholic Church where my immigrant grandparents attended. The services were always spoken entirely in Ukrainian for the benefit of the Ukrainian immigrants who attended. Not one single English word was spoken so I had no idea what was being said. So most of the time, I simply tuned out and tuned *into* my own personal relationship with my Beloved as I sat through the two-hour service.

You could say that I am a blank slate for my Beloved to work within me in ways that I would perceive to be extremely personal, and not complicated by religious dogma. Perhaps this simple way of "knowing" of my Beloved's Grace is why I feel so compelled to answer whatever call I am being asked. I trust my Source above all else. At times we are like trees bending together as though whispering secrets.

So I poured myself into learning all I could about the very rare unitive experience. From sunup until sundown, I read books on mysticism, the mystics, and the saints. At times my eyes strained from reading so much material. But I knew this book was supposed to be written. I knew that my Beloved would take me there as long as I followed the natural impulse of my soul to move past my uncertainties and open myself to where God wants to lead me.

While I find it is important to remain humble when writing about my sacred experiences, I realize there may be a tendency for others to judge me as being a spiritual narcissist, one whose ego is inflated when it comes to my own spiritual experiences and wisdom. Truthfully, anyone who knows me can vouch that my life is all about GOD, and being a servant to help lift people's hearts closer to God in some way. It's NOT about me. No matter how strongly I feel about expressing the Divine Grace that appeared in my life, I know these gifts weren't given to me because I earned them in any way.

I am a very simple woman who loves God above all. I would never betray that love for self-glorification. I must write as I was "told" by my Great Teacher, the Light, to write what was revealed to me. I must use words to try to convey the impossible mystery with the hope that in doing so, someone will be inspired to draw closer to God and to know the joy of loving and being loved by Him.

My greatest desire is that this book will inspire others to lift their hearts closer to the Divine Presence within. Without question, honoring the One who has gifted me is the most sacred responsibility of my time on earth. Often, we learn more from first person accounts of someone's journey to God and the fruits received from traveling that road. Expect nothing from this book except a willingness to open your mind with a sincere desire to give yourself totally to God. There is no other purpose. If what I write within the pages of this book flames one's own heart with the possibility and consuming desire to be more, then I would not tamper in the slightest with what God has revealed to me during my unitive experience. I would sooner fall down physically dead on the spot, than to compromise the message of what God has given to me. There is no agenda – absolutely none – in my writing, except to express the best I can what God has revealed.

Think of this book as being a road map toward God, toward *knowing* a life in which the great fear of death, the total annihilation of self does not have to hold power over us. More so, there is a way out of life's heartaches and suffering. It consists of finding man's true identity, the Divine Presence within. One must be willing to listen, and to learn something new, for our life transformation is in exact proportion to the amount of truth we can accept without running away. To the degree that we learn to live from our true inner self, will we then know the sacred way of life bearing the fruits of love, understanding, compassion, and lessening our fears and suffering.

If you keep your heart open throughout these pages, then I am sure that your own experience will convince you that the reality I speak of is far greater than what I have told you.

I will also be sharing some of the writings that some mystics and saints wrote about their experiences of God. I hope to convey their profound intellect and hearts as they pierced into God's true nature. These personal experiences as handed down through the centuries, are all we can truly know of our Beloved.

The mystics' and saints' voices are so beautiful that I feel unable to articulate my own voice as poignantly as theirs, thus relying on their quotes to convey what I want to say. After all, they experienced a sense of absolute completeness, of oneness with God that only comes from having the soul's full awareness restored. As someone who, by God's grace allowed my own soul to be awakened to the highest reality in union with God, I have selected the mystics' and saints' quotes that are relative to my own personal experience.

The mystics and saints knew their visions did not take place "out there" in our physical world. Their "knowing" process was directed inward as opposed to being determined by outer sources, such as churches and religious dogma.

They knew that to get to the hidden God, they had to undertake a journey of the soul. The inner realm became the avenue to the Divine. They opened the door to the ultimate, transcendent God, paving the way for us to be able to open that door as well. They would understand the One as not limited by form, present in all things, and changeless. Their eyes would see through His eyes, and they would comprehend His eternity as their own.

As I poured through the literature of the mystics and saints, I was often, overcome with sheer JOY, as if love danced upon my soul on all sides like millions of diamonds. I understood their words because I inwardly experienced them as well. Their beautiful words touched my essence and brought me "home" again to savor my Beloved's inner Presence. The warmth of His Love within me brought forth such sweet fragrances of bliss cascading to my consciousness as gentle as the flower gives off its perfume.

So when reading the quotes of some of the mystics and saints I have chosen to include in this book, allow each one as I did, to percolate slowly. Sometimes the beautiful illuminated words will begin to subtly move into your heart crying forth the same love that kissed the saint. It will be the same love that is hidden in you and kissed by God.

I hope that in contributing the wisdom my Great Teacher also revealed to me will bring you the comforting message of a new way of thinking so that you may realize the truth about yourself and be what you truly are – one at all times with the Divine. All you need is within. Know this, and your guidance will be true, will replenish you, will guide you, and will prosper the purpose for which you are on earth. As you stay in tune with the Source within you, your daily life will take care of itself easily. As you ask for help and guidance, no matter the adversity in your life, that help will be there.

*"I will soothe you and heal you; I will bring you roses.
I too, have been covered with thorns."*

- Rumi

Nancy Clark

CHAPTER 1
WHO ARE THE MYSTICS AND THE SAINTS

We have the opportunity to look into the mystics' and saints' hearts to discover our own longings for our Beloved. It isn't enough simply to be curious about their visions, ecstasies, and apparitions and wanting those as well. If we can look beyond the curiosity, we discover the beauty of a unitive love between God and a person. I believe their love for God first and foremost, gave birth to their extraordinary revelations and consolations of His Presence.

Many saints were incredibly intuitive, allowing them to recognize God's voice or presence in ways or places that many others wouldn't be aware. They also suffered from physical, emotional and spiritual darkness at times. Thus, they were very sensitive to the sufferings of others and were drawn to reach out to them with God's healing comfort. Their sufferings were considered a spiritual gift for that reason. It takes great compassion and love to reach out to another while one is suffering oneself.

Because they lived to please God throughout their lives, they were steeped in humility. Even though they received great visions, they never experienced delusions of grandeur. In fact, many did not talk about their experiences for fear of ridicule or terrible persecutions during that early time period. We can learn from their spirituality how we can deepen our own interior spiritual development starting from humility, love and compassion. Without love, one does not deserve to be called a mystic.

I have selected several mystics and saints who represent my own unitive experience and the wisdom received when the Spirit of God within opened to my consciousness and brought about the depth and breadth of the glory of God within.

I had dissolved in union with the Divine by Divine Grace and sent back to physical consciousness with a calling to help others awaken to their true nature. Had I not been asked to fulfill this calling from God, I would have remained quiet about having had this blessed encounter with our Beloved. I would have simply held the experience with great humility dear to my heart and lived the transformed life quietly. But that is not what I was called to do. I accepted my destiny to "speak and write" what my Great Teacher revealed to me no matter the cost.

In studying the mystics and the saints, it became clear to me that some in particular spoke to my inner being with a love and voice that became like a magnetic pull, deeper into my own inner abiding with God. It is my hope that the mystics and saints I have chosen to acknowledge within these pages will also bring you an awareness of the inviting nature of the Divine within.

A brief description of the mystics and saints whose beautiful quotes I use include:

SAINT TERESA OF AVILA

Saint Teresa was a Carmelite nun who was very independent. She established small convents throughout Spain traveling on foot. Thus, she became known as the "walking saint." She began to have visions of Jesus which led her to focus her writings upon the ascent of the soul towards God. She taught her nuns to think and pray on their own, and to concentrate in order to hear the Lord in their interior, in what she called the "Interior Castle." Her best known book on mysticism, is *The Interior Castle* written in 1588. The book is based on her profound personal experience of ecstasy. Saint Teresa says the soul goes through four stages in its ascent towards God.

Stage One is called the Devotion of the Heart. Through deep mental prayer, and through great effort and concentration, the person begins to pray on Christ's passion.

Stage Two is called the Devotion of Peace. Here, God gives a special grace of quiet and peace to the person even if there are distractions. Peace remains.

Stage Three is called the Devotion of Union. God gives the person the gift of becoming united with Him in that their reason is completely merged into Him and the only thing left that the person can control is their memory and imagination.

Stage Four is called the Devotion of Ecstasy. Here, the person is granted the gift of God's grace and is totally unaware of their own self and their own body. The person is completely merged into oneness with God. (Unitive Experience.)

The only stage humans can reach on their own with their own discipline and effort is the first stage. The other three stages are all given by God's grace, and to those people who are very spiritually mature. Most people never achieve this unitive experience during their lifetimes.

3

SAINT AUGUSTINE

Saint Augustine, 354-430, also known as Augustine of Hippo was a Roman African who was not a particular moral person before his conversion experience. He struggled with his sinful transgressions. Writing about his youth, he reflected, *"Our real pleasure consisted in doing something that was forbidden. The evil in me was foul, but I loved it."*

One day he heard a voice in his head saying, *"Take up and read."* He picked up the bible lying on a table and read the first thing he saw. *"Not in reveling and drunkenness, not in lust and wantonness, not in quarrels and rivalries. Rather, arm yourselves with the Lord Jesus Christ, spend no more thought on nature and nature's appetites." (Romans 13:13-14).*

That convinced him to leave his career as a professional public speaker and teacher of rhetoric in order to dedicate his life to God. He became the bishop of Hippo and spent the next 35 years preaching, celebrating mass, and ministering to his congregation.

He became a prolific writer, producing more than 300 sermons, 500 letters, and other works. He wrote an account of his conversion in *Confessions*, a set of 13 books in Latin in which he gave an account of his conversion to Christianity.

Besides that famous work, his other classic work is, the *City of God*. Saint Augustine was very influential on the development of Christianity.

EVELYN UNDERHILL

Evelyn Underhill, 1875-1941, was an English Angio-Catholic writer, mystic, pacifist, laywoman affiliated with no religious order. She left behind no movement, institution, or organization. She was however, considered one of the most highly read writers on the subject of Christian mysticism and spirituality.

Throughout her long and prolific career as a writer, spiritual director, and retreat conductor, she devoted her entire ministry to helping others into a new way of understanding the love of God and how God can make a difference in our lives. She published 39 books and numerous articles. She was best known for her book *Mysticism*, published in 1911.

Evelyn Underhill speaks to us from the past, but offers timeless wisdom that can illuminate and even transform our lives today.

RUMI

Jalal ad-Din Mohammad Rumi, 1207-1273, was a Persian poet, mystic, Sufi, theologian, and scholar. Rumi's discovery of poetry is attributed to his friendship with a mystic who preached the possibility and necessity of direct communion with God. It was after his friendship with this mystic ended; some believed he was cast out of the town by jealous sons of Rumi, that Rumi's poetry began to become prolific. His poems came from dealing with separation, love, the source of creation, and out of facing death. He saw every form of human love as a mirror of the Divine. Rumi's poetry sold millions of copies, making him the most popular poet in the US and around the world.

SAINT JOHN OF THE CROSS

Saint John of the Cross, 1542-1591, was one of the greatest Christian mystics and Spanish poets, doctor of the church, and cofounder of the contemplative order of Discalced Carmelites with Saint Teresa of Avila. He was imprisoned twice due to friction in the order. It was there where he wrote some of his finest poetry. His best work was *Dark Night of the Soul*, where he expresses the experience of mystical union between the soul and Christ. In his book, he describes the process by which the soul loses its attachment to everything, resulting in a personal experience of union with the Beloved.

THERESE OF LISIEUX

Saint Therese of Lisieux, 1873-1897, a French Catholic is perhaps one of the most known and best loved saints. At age 14, she had an experience with God, transforming her life forever. At age 15, she entered the convent giving her whole life to God. She was gifted with great intimacy with God and lived each day with an unshakable confidence in God's love even though she suffered greatly with tuberculosis. "What matters in life," she wrote, "is not great deeds, but great love. She loved flowers and saw herself as the "little flower of Jesus," who gave glory to God just by being her small self among all the other beautiful flowers in God's garden. "My mission-to make God loved – will begin after my death." She said, "I will spend my heaven doing good on earth. I will let fall a shower of roses." Roses have been described and experienced as Saint Therese's signature character. She died at the young age of twenty –four.

RAINER MARIA RILKE

Rainer Maria Rilke, 1875- 1926, was an Austrian German Poet. He was one of the most gifted and conscientious artists who ever lived. He lived on the brink of poverty for much of his life. He led a solitary life wandering from person to person and from place to place. The people he met offered him the emotional support he needed. At one time he became a friend and worked as a secretary for the great artist Rodin.

His works have been described as inherently "mystical" which dealt with beautiful metaphors for life and love. Whenever he wrote about God, he doesn't refer to God in the traditional sense, but rather uses the term to refer to the life force or nature. Rilke is often quoted or referenced in the entertainment media when these works discuss the subject of love or angels.

YUNUS EMRE

Yunus Emre, 1238-1320, was a Turkish poet and Sufi mystic who was a very lonely man since childhood. The more lonely and sorrowful he became, the more compassionate he became to others who suffered. He traveled from village to village on foot seeking out those individuals who were starving and prayed to God that he could be used to help alleviate their suffering.

During his travels he gathered food for those who were starving. He is said to have spoken these words which reveal his compassion: "Let me go into the world with my solitude, my otherness, I will become an intimate friend of those who sorrow."

His poems never separated himself from the reality of those who suffer. His poems explained very profound truths but he was able to explain them in a language making it easier to understand for the people in his day.

SAINT RABI'S AL-ADAWLYYA

Rabi's al-Adawlyya, 713-801, was a female Muslim saint and Sufi mystic. An orphan, she was sold into slavery. One day she ran away from her owner. Falling on her knees she called out to God saying, *"All I want is for You to be pleased with me, to know whether You are pleased with me or not."* She heard a reply reassuring her not to be sad and that everything would be okay. She then ran back to her owner.

One night her owner heard her praying. He saw a chainless lantern suspended over her head which lit up the entire room. The owner freed her after witnessing that and she spent the rest of her life in devotion to God.

She lived for God. Her only concern was God. She reached a state which all Sufi's strive for through the destruction of her ego/self. Her relationship with God was built on love and trust, seeking only to please God for love itself, not for any desires for reward.

SUMNUN THE LOVER

Sumnun al-Muhibb (Sumnun the Lover) was a Sufi mystic from Baghdad. He was known for his beliefs that love is the foundation and principle of the way to God. He held to the belief that all the various mystical states and spiritual practices are of a lesser way to full knowledge of God. He believed that every spiritual practice that the seeker practices is susceptible to faltering as long as it remains in existence. But love is not susceptible whatsoever to decline as long as it remains in existence.

All other Sufi masters are in total agreement with him concerning love. Sumnun's most famous statement about love was, *"A thing can be explained only by means of something more subtle than itself, and since there is nothing subtler than love, by what, then can one explain it?"*

RUTH BURROWS

Ruth Burrows is known as Sister Rachel in her Carmelite community in Norfolk, UK. She has authored several mystical best-selling books including, *Before the Living God and Essence of Prayer*. She is considered one of the great, and deep spiritual writers of our time. Ruth Burrows is her pen name.

ELIE WIESEL

Elie Wiesel, 1928 – 2016, was a Romanian-born American Jewish professor, political activist, Nobel-Prize winning author, and Holocaust survivor. After surviving the Holocaust, Elie wrote the internationally acclaimed memoir *Night*. He also wrote many other books and became a great speaker, speaking out against persecution and injustice across the world.

DIONYSIUS THE AREOPAGITE

Dionysius the Areopagite lived around the 1st century A.D. He was converted to Christianity by the Apostle Paul after hearing Paul's sermons. Dionysius became the Bishop of Athens and became a Christian writer. His mystical writings taught that seeking God with one's entire being was the only thing worth seeking. He insisted that God Himself was the soul itself, and that there was an inward way to God available to all men.

For him, personal experience was the primary essence in religion that transcended mere head-knowledge. Finding God with one's whole being and with one's whole heart, will and mind even if language could not explain what was experienced.

SAI BABA

Bhagavan Sri Sathya Sai Baba was born in 1926 in India. He is inspiring millions of people worldwide by his personal example to live the ideal that "service to man is service to God." He is said to be "pure love walking on two feet." The fundamental truth of man's divine nature is at the heart of his message and mission.

In his own words, *"I have come not to disturb or destroy any faith, but to confirm each in his own faith, so that the Christian becomes a better Christian, the Muslim, a better Muslim, and the Hindu, a better Hindu."*

SOCRATES

Socrates was born in 470 BC in Athens, Greece and died at age seventy-one. He was a great philosopher who is credited with being the founder of Western philosophy. He believed that philosophy based on ethical human reason rather than theological doctrine would result in a greater well-being of society.

He believed that the better one knows himself, the better able one is able to reason and make choices that will bring true happiness. He always emphasized the importance of the mind over the unimportance of the human body. His famous quote is, *"the unexamined life is not worth living."*

SAINT THOMAS AQUINAS

Saint Thomas Aquinas, 1225-1274, was an Italian Dominican theologian, philosopher, and an authority of the Roman Catholic Church. After completing his education, St. Thomas Aquinas devoted himself to a life of traveling, writing, teaching, public speaking, and preaching. His writings became a great influence world-wide among seminaries, colleges, universities, and among common men and women. He is best known for his five logical arguments regarding the existence of God in his book *Summa Theologiciae.*

Those who knew Saint Thomas Aquinas were said to have reported that he received assistance from heaven. To Father Reginald he said that he learned more in prayer and contemplation than he had acquired from man or books. It is also reported that the Blessed Virgin Mary appeared to him to assure him that his life and his writings were acceptable to God and that he would persevere in his calling. Saint Peter and Paul, and Saint Dominic also visited him in visions.

One day in 1273, Saint Thomas Aquinas had a mystical vision that made writing seem no longer relevant to him. While at mass, he heard a voice coming from a crucifix that said, "Thou hast written well of me Thomas; what reward wilt thou have?" Saint Thomas Aquinas replied, *"None other than thyself, Lord."*

From that moment on, he no longer wrote again. When pressured to write, he replied, *"I can do no more. Such secrets have been revealed to me that all I have written now appears to be of little value."*

11

J. KRISHNAMURTI

Krishnamurti, 1895-1986 was an Indian philosopher, speaker, and writer on psychological, sociological, and spiritual subjects. His teachings dealt with the nature of the human mind, consciousness, meditation, and human relationships. He believed that personal transformation could only be brought about by a holistic transformation from within. All the answers to our human condition are not to be found elsewhere he believed, but within ourselves.

He believed life itself was God, and every action manifested itself with God. He traveled throughout the world speaking about the need for a radical change in mankind. He didn't belong to any religious organization nor did he put his faith into any school of political or ideological thought. He felt these are the very factors that divide human beings and bring about conflict. He reminds us that we are all human beings first and not different from one another. Krishnamurti authored about forty books.

MOTHER ANGELICA

Mother Angelica, 1923-2016, was born in Canton, Ohio. In her teenage years she suffered a severe stomach ailment. A mystic suggested she call upon Saint Therese for help in healing. When she realized that God loved her immensely and brought her through her incredible recovery, she resolved to give herself totally to God and become a nun.

In 1981, Mother Angelica launched Eternal Word Television Network with only $200.00 for start-up costs. Year after year she found opportunities for giving spiritual talks, writing, and printing Mini-Books. The television program she produced and was featured in became a Catholic

Multimedia Enterprise turning it into one of the world's largest religious media-operations.

BROTHER WAYNE TEASDALE

Wayne Teasdale, 1945-2004, was a Catholic monk, mystic, author and teacher. He knew at an early age that he would grow up to become a priest. During the turbulent sixties, he was challenged in his belief in the goodness of God, which plunged him into a three-year-long "dark night of the soul."

During this dark period in his life, he met and became friends with Father Thomas Keating. That friendship opened up the mystical dimension of Teasdale's life. Teasdale dedicated his life to seeing the commonality and common wisdom which could be found in all of the world's great religions.

Based on his understanding of this reality of all religious traditions, he coined the term, "interspirituality." Interspirituality is about love and oneness and the sanctity of all things. It sees all religious experience and spiritual paths as one evolutionary process and the ultimate potential of our species.

SADHGURU

Sadhguru, born 1957 is a spiritual reformer, mystic, and New York Times bestselling author. In 1982 he had a mystical experience of being one with everything, the rock he was sitting on, the air – everything. Following his experience he travelled extensively in an effort to gain insight into his experience. He went on to develop yoga classes, which led him to establish the Isha Foundation, a non-profit organization which hosts a series of programs to heighten self-awareness through yoga.

SAINT JEAN BAPTISTE MARIE VIANNEY

Saint Jean Baptiste Marie Vianney, 1786 – 1859, was a French priest who was internationally known for his priestly work in his parish. It is reported about 20,000 persons visited him every year from the time he became a priest until he died to make their confessions to him. He spent as many as 12 or 15 hours daily in his confessional.

CHAPTER 2
WHAT IS THE
UNITIVE EXPERIENCE?

Yikes! What a project I undertook when I answered God's call to write about the unitive experience! I did not know what the word meant, let alone be able to describe it so others would understand what this enormous gift of grace was that I received. I wondered how in the world I would accomplish this project. I spent months researching the literature to find examples of the unitive experience, an experience where only God is present. In my vast readings in Christian literature, I found definitions that spoke of "union in Christ" that were being loosely thrown around to include such forms as a close relationship with God, through prayer, through a personal sense that God is with the subject and so on. But that is not the unitive experience that I had, whereby I had merged into complete oneness with God and there was no "self." Only God was present. Apparently this is the highest state of being and is very, very rare, and only attained by the greatest of saints and mystics. **I want to be very clear, I was not a saint before my unitive experience nor did I become a saint afterwards!**

In a personal conversation with a former monk, he told me, *"Every aspirant who has ever attempted to describe the unitive experience knows there is no alphabet that vast. You have tasted Unity. The source of your being dissolved into Unity, into God. It is bigger than the biggest and smaller than the smallest. There is no observer. There is only God, and you are that. Jesus said, 'the Father and I are one.' He may have been the only character in the New Testament to have known the unitive experience."*

At times some of the saints and mystics hinted at having had a unitive experience, but it was difficult for me to recognize their descriptions. They tended to be poetic and metaphoric. I also learned that even the monks that 'do this for a living' don't describe it with much detail.

Studying the mystical literature also presented some problems. There are lots of accounts of people having an experience of seeing God while transcending the physical dimension during rest, sitting in a chair, dreams, watching a sunset, near-death experiences or other spiritually transformative experiences. At times, these experiences caused such feelings of bliss, peace, and an overwhelming sense of being loved. People having these experiences often speak of experiencing union with the cosmos, the Light, and humanity, however, they remain cognizant of the union. The union is not total, for the experience happens without the loss of the ego "I." When the loss of the ego "I" as the witness occurs, this state of oneness is called non-dual consciousness, or unitive consciousness.

Unitive consciousness described by Jesus in the tenth chapter of John's gospel is, *"I and the father are one."* That is the highest level of non-duality, the highest level of seeing. Unitive consciousness is the state in which pure Divine knowledge is revealed by God, arising in pure love of God and for God. Pure Divine knowledge cannot be revealed by theology or study because this type of knowledge is limited, no matter how brilliant the human faculties are. Pure Divine knowledge cannot be received through intuition or inspiration because this is subjective and veiled by human nature.

While in a state of grace, God removes all veils within the human that would hinder sight and understanding so that pure Divine knowledge is experienced directly. God's Divine nature is revealed in a manner which prohibits doubt. The human condition of fear, awe, wonder, reasoning, and even human love ceases. Only the attributes of God are known. This is the highest ascent that can be known. There is no other ascent possible. There is simply the passing away from the self into God. The knowledge of the true meaning of the soul's unification with God comes to be known. This comes as a gift from God; no human can manifest this unitive gift by some method on our part. By following the mystical path however, the soul can become more aware of itself as part of the Divine Soul thereby experiencing a very real and vital relationship between the soul and the living God.

St. John of the Cross wrote:

"In thus allowing God to work in it, the soul...is at once illumined and transformed in God, and God communicates to it His supernatural Being, in such ways that it appears to be God Himself, and has all that God Himself has. And this union comes to pass when God grants the soul this supernatural favour, that all the things of God and the soul are one in participant transformation; and the soul seems to be God rather than a soul, and is indeed God by participation; although it is true that its natural

17

being, though thus transformed, is as distinct from the Being of God as it was before."

From my study of individuals who had spiritually transformative experiences and documented in my book, ***Divine Moments: Ordinary People Having Spiritually Transformative Experiences***, one woman wrote: *"Suddenly, I was immersed, surrounded, embraced in golden, oceanic, Light, full of peace and love, joy, fulfillment, of being Home. When my vision ended, my face was drenched in tears. My heart changed."* She claimed that God had spoken to her.

One man wrote, *"I saw the Light and radiating from it was pure white. I knew it was God. Only God could emanate such glorious love."*

Another man wrote, *"At some point, a most incredible light becomes present. It is not normal light; it is an all-consuming 'living' light-presence/personage, and it just radiates all things and all love in it. I realized that this Divine Light is God. It is incredibly evident; it is known to you as soon as you are in its presence. There is no doubt. You want to be in that presence forever and never leave."*

These examples, while very beautiful and life-transforming for the individuals having those experiences, are not unitive experiences. They are mystical visions which means someone was present to perceive the vision and the apparition was present. The only qualifier for a unitive experience is that only God is present. In the case of a unitive experience, it is union with God, not the ocean, the cosmos, everyone on the planet, **but with God, and** *seeing from God's vision or consciousness.* **The ego 'I' self is not present to observe anything that is occurring. Only God is present.**

A simple way of understanding the difference between a mystical experience and a unitive experience is this. A mystical experience is *seeing* oneness, while a unitive experience is seeing *from* oneness.

> *"I have felt myself caught up in such intimacy that it seemed as if I were melting into Him-as if He were one flame, and I was one small flame, and we were joined at the wick, where it's white light and the heat melts and the two flames are swallowed into one."*
>
> —St. Teresa of Avila

Brother Wayne Teasdale, is a lay interreligious monk and mystic. He describes his unitive experience when he was an undergraduate at St. Anselm College in New Hampshire.

> *"I was drawn beyond myself into a place not of this world."* He experienced everything being united with the *"Divine One."* Notice how he explains his vision when his ego was gone. *"Standing on the bare ground, my head bathed by the blithe air, and uplifted into infinite space – all mean egotism vanishes. I become a transparent eyeball. I am nothing. I see all. The currents of the Universal Being circulate through me. I am part or particle of God."*

John writes in the Ascent of Mount Carmel:

> *"When God grants this supernatural favor to the soul, so great a union is caused that all the things of both God and the soul become one in participant transformation, and the soul appears to be God more than a soul. Indeed, it is God by participation yet truly, its being (even the*

transformed) is naturally and distinct from God's as it was before, just as the window, although illumined by the ray, has an existence distinct from the ray."

St. Teresa of Avila said of her unitive experience,

"It would come upon me unexpectedly so that I could in no way doubt He was within me or I totally immersed in Him." She continues, "It seemed to me there came the thought of how a sponge absorbs and is saturated with water; so, I thought, was my soul, which was overflowing with that divinity and in a certain way rejoicing within itself and possessing the three Persons. I also heard the words: "Don't try to hold Me within yourself, but try to hold yourself within Me."

Rumi wrote,

"First he pampered me with a hundred favors, then he melted me with the fire of sorrows; after he sealed me with the seal of love, I became Him, then he threw myself out of me."

One near-death experiencer described his unitive experience this way.

"The light was in me and between the molecules, the cells in my body. He was in me – I was in him....I knew all things. I saw all things. I was all things. But not me; Jesus had this. As long as I was "in Him" and He was "in me," I had this power, this glory."

Another person described his experience while awake and not close to death, suddenly being taken into the Light-Being. *"I felt Him IN me, my forehead, my face, my heart, my body, everything!"* The person described losing *"complete consciousness of myself,"* and feeling *"like He washed me from the inside."*

Perhaps one more example from St. Catherine of Siena will help you to better understand the impact of having the unitive experience.

"They are like the burning coal that no one can put out once it is completely consumed in the furnace, because it has itself been turned into fire. So it is with these souls cast into the furnace of my charity, who keep nothing at all, not a bit of their own will, outside of me but are completely set afire in me. There is no one who can seize them or drag them out of my grace. They have been made one with me and I with them."

When my own unitive experience ended and I returned to self-consciousness and the ego-I present, I was able to recall what took place during those moments when my Spirit –being was lost in the Divine Presence. My soul had been given its freedom to be what its true nature was during that sacred experience – one with God. From that moment, my life was transformed into wanting nothing more than to love God above all, to do the will of God, and to help others lift their hearts closer to Him in some way. I see this as my life's purpose.

I keep asking myself why did I have such a sacred experience with the Creator? I am an ordinary and simple woman. Why would I be called to write about being awakened into unitive consciousness when I never heard the word before, let alone write about this inner dimension that awakened and ascended me inward into the kingdom of God?

Trust me, had I not been called "to speak and write" what my Great Teacher revealed to me during those Sacred moments with Him, I would **never** call attention to myself – never! I would not want to be regarded as being holier-than-thou or denounced as being blasphemous. This encounter with my Beloved was for me, a very holy and sacred experience that was so very private to me. The last thing I would want to do is to shout it from the rooftops and call attention to myself. The Sacredness of this experience was just between God and me. However, my Beloved had different plans for me. I was told to "speak and write" what my Beloved called me to do, and I am keeping my promise to serve.

From that instant, I knew that I would spend the rest of my days devoted to serving God in the manner I was called. I promised to serve until I draw my final breath. Yes, I answered the call for the sake of love, of accountability, and of service. From day one of my unitive experience with my Beloved, I have sought and have worked to be a loving instrument of Divine will. It's all about God, not me!

I returned from that experience a changed person. I feel my Beloved's presence with me every day being revealed to me as I listen to the quieter inner voice of Spirit which blesses every aspect of my life. Appreciating each moment as it comes and resting in it, brings a sense of well-being.

However, even though I was in a state of pure Divine consciousness for some time, I returned back to the ego-mind mentality where my self-centered nature operates on a daily basis. It seems afterwards, I became as sensitive as a barometer, sometimes becoming agitated like a storm-tossed ship when I learn of the political issues of the day for instance. I find that I must turn the TV news off so I don't become so upset. I can then revert back to experiencing the softness of my inner life.

Seeing the mallard ducks eating the goldfish in my garden pond prompts me to run like a wild-woman after the ducks yelling at them to stop killing the fish, only to sit down on the bench seat and cry as if an undefined sadness has fallen around me like a dark rain cloud. Because I am very sensitive, I feel disillusioned and cry out when some who have tasted mystical experiences with the Light, can sometimes be cruel to others.

There are a myriad of events that can lessen my awareness of my peaceful inner true nature. I'm human after all, with an ego still intact. I accept all the idiosyncrasies of selfhood. I haven't evolved spiritually where I am living permanently in the unitive state which is an irreversible change of consciousness *into* Christ Consciousness. But I tasted it, and I now understand that this highest state of Being is what humanity is evolving toward, me included. The only way toward our evolvement and ultimate new humanity is a change of consciousness, a transcendence of the false sense of self whereby God becomes the total outward expression of the Divine within us.

Richard Maurice Bucke, M.D.'s book, *Cosmic Consciousness* is a remarkable study first published in 1901. It is a classic investigation of the development of man's mystic relation to the Infinite. He wrote: *"Deep in the soul, below pain, below all the distraction of life, is a silence vast and grand - an infinite ocean of calm, which nothing can disturb; Nature's own exceeding peace, which "passes understanding.""*This is the state I seek when my own lower ego-self is trying to control my state of affairs. That is why I always turn inward to my constant companion – the Divine Presence who seems always to be on call. Immediately, I am offered the peaceful stillness, moment to moment, or a sign of what I need to do to see whatever is disturbing me from a different perspective.

Transformation of our lower consciousness is what we must all strive for so that ultimately, humanity will have cleared a path for the Sacred to appear thus, transforming our world. We will then realize the human condition as being 'heaven on earth.' Perhaps the only reason why I was invited by God's Grace to have had the unitive experience was simply to bear witness and to testify what is possible for humanity to achieve –transforming union with the Sacred. Those who listen to the call of the Spirit within to spread the seed of love everywhere will give birth to new races and new nations. The sacred love is encoded in every cell of every human body, creating, growing, arranging. A day will come when we will become stewards of a new holy human life because we chose to embark upon the transition that lies ahead, awaiting us.

CHAPTER 3
MY UNITIVE EXPERIENCE

In the norm of everyday life, everything operates from self-centeredness where one's ego reinforces a view of reality as a separate and unique entity. January 29, 1979 was a day in which my ego was extinguished and I instantaneously awakened *into* God. There was only God taking the shape of the totality of my experience from moment to moment, of and in God. This was a gift of God's grace of unspeakable ecstasy. It was not something within my human control, but rather something by grace I received.

That cold wintry morning, my family and I awoke feeling shattered like broken glass. Our dear friend John had died in a plane crash and we were preparing to attend his funeral service. His wife Jean had asked me to write and deliver the eulogy but I was too emotionally wrought with grief to consider delivering the eulogy. Instead, I agreed to write the eulogy and the minister agreed to deliver that message.

Once at the funeral home, everyone was gathering and extending condolences to our friend's family. The beautiful flowers that lined his casket and around the room were wafting their fragrances as if breathing compassion into our hearts for the great loss that so many of us felt that morning.

Approximately fifteen minutes before the start of the service, I began to feel something I never felt before in my entire life. I was standing next to Jean at the time when suddenly, a very strong and powerful surge of energy began to travel from the tips of my toes, moving upwards along my spine. It was like a great express train, roaring, flashing, dashing, headlong up to the top of my head where it then exited. Immediately, I felt as if a thousand helium balloons were attached to my shoulders, lifting every worry, fear and concern away from my body. The peace that flowed through my body was an unearthly peace, unlike anything I have ever experienced before. The best words ever written to describe that feeling are, *"I am leaving you with a gift – peace of mind and heart! And the peace I give isn't fragile like the peace the world gives."* (John 14:27). In some secret place deep within me, my grief became faint and distant as the light of the sun that had long set.

I don't believe Jean noticed anything happening to me at that time. She simply said, *"The minister will start the service in a few minutes and will deliver the eulogy."* *"No, Jean, I have to be the one to deliver the eulogy,"* I told her. Confused, she said, *"What do you mean? You said you couldn't handle delivering the eulogy."* I replied, *"Yes, I can. In fact, I have to be the one to deliver the eulogy."* I spoke with authority, my lips forming those words as if a wiser part of me were speaking. I had no conscious idea why I said it had to be me. Up until that very moment, I was intent upon the minister delivering the eulogy. In retrospect, I believe I acted solely on the prompting of Spirit's Holy Voice within, preparing me for the unitive experience I would soon receive.

It took several years before I learned what that tremendous and powerful energy that traveled up my spine and exited out the top of my head was. That energy is called kundalini energy. Apparently, this energy lies dormant in the human body at the base of the spine. When this energy is awakened, the kundalini travels through the different chakras, leading to different levels of spiritual awakening until the energy finally reaches the top of the head. There, it produces profound transformation of consciousness. Sometimes kundalini *exits* the top of the head as it did in my case. That's where it initiates an extremely powerful transformation of consciousness, in which duality ceases.

The subject of kundalini is vast and I prefer not to delve into the phenomena at this time. For those interested however, I would refer you to the Kundalini Research Network, www.kundalininet.org for more information.

At that time in my life, I had no knowledge of esoteric or spiritual matters. The only books I read were cookbooks, medical, and gardening books that helped to nurture my ordinary life. I was no different than any other everyday wife, mother, career woman, and friend. I could easily have been your next door neighbor. Life was simple for me. But January 29, 1979 was the beginning of a new life for me – a chance to live the true life I came here to live. I would be set free to see it, to know it, and to follow it increasingly.

The kundalini experience that day set everything in motion. Once I told Jean that I had to be the one to deliver the eulogy, she quickly alerted the minister that I would deliver the eulogy. As I started to walk toward the lectern, and just before approaching it, I sensed John's spirit beside me. I felt my right hand being placed in his hand. Reacting to his "presence," I turned my head to my right as if to acknowledge him. No, I didn't see John with my physical eyes, but I "saw" him through some supernatural manner. I absolutely knew he was holding my hand and reassuring me that he was very happy!

My plan was to simply read the words I had written for the eulogy. My body was very relaxed; grief was non-existent. I began to read the words on the paper in front of me when suddenly, my eyes lifted toward the rear of the room. From ceiling level, there appeared a brilliant white Light that radiated unspeakable radiance. No, it wasn't overhead light fixtures. This Light was hallowed and unearthly, like an infinite number of suns and stars merged into one living Being, calling me unto Itself. The brilliance of the Light staggered my comprehension because I was able to see this Light without squinting or my physical eyes being injured. My eyes blazed and glowed in the golden Light like a mosaic of a hundred thousand jewels.

The moment I saw the Light, I knew "Who" the Light was. The same Light that I encountered during my near-death experience during childbirth years earlier was once more illuminating my consciousness. Every cell in my body reacted to the Light's Presence. Blissful joy, love, gratitude, awe, reverence, and humility were the emotions I felt. An ecstasy which suddenly overwhelmed me, I realized I was once again, in the presence of God. My heart bowed down like violets after rain; humility was consuming my soul.

Powerfully, yet gently, my spirit-self or soul lifted out of my physical body like a whirlwind, and merged into oneness with the Light-God. Throughout the entire fifteen minutes it took me to deliver the eulogy, my physical body was engaged in that physical activity. To everyone in the audience, I appeared normally, delivering a eulogy. However, my spirit-self had transcended the physical limitation of the earth plane and entered a higher realm with the Light-God.

As if a door were suddenly left ajar into some world unseen before, the fullness of my essence revealed there to be no distinction between self and God. My union with God burnt like living coals in my soul, burning with unspeakable, pure love. The impurities of the coals in my soul were cast out, leaving behind the precious diamonds previously hidden. I became pure as God Himself because I was united in **oneness** with God. I lived in God; I saw and understood through God. My ego was non-existent.

During the entire time I was united in oneness with God, I was able to *be* pure, unconditional love. It was not love of this earthly realm where we place conditions on the love we give to others. Love me, and I'll love you. No, this was love without conditions. The love *was* God. An indescribable euphoria that extended beyond human comprehension had intermingled with the Light's blissful Love as I was being welcomed "home."

I had emerged from this physical world of illusion into the *real* reality, understanding nothing on my own, but comprehending everything that God represents. The realm I found myself in, was a soft, soothing, and gentle mystery, like the whisper of a child murmuring its happiness in its sleep. I was "home" and cradled in the arms of my Heavenly Father with nary a concern.

Time and space were non-existent during the entire time of my experience. Everything happened simultaneously. Communication was instantly understood; there were no questions to be asked, for I knew the answer immediately. Something *beyond* the known, the mystery of the unknown had revealed itself to me in that moment of oneness with the Light-God.

My soul's trajectory into the Being of Light, in which the highest form of love was encountered, was the feeling of ecstasy, as my entire being was consumed with the very Presence of the Creator. I had no delusions about what I was experiencing. All my previous beliefs and convictions were seemingly being erased like a snowflake lost in the ocean as I stood united before the Creator in all my innocence.

A pure Spirit, my consciousness was elevated to know the Divine nature of myself. The luminous quality of the radiance within was so overwhelmingly beautiful to me! Wonderful concepts of truth were being fed into my mind from a heightened spiritual splendor, winging their way to me with lucid wisdom, and revealing to me all that I had forgotten while my soul had been inhabiting a physical body on earth.

I was remembering truths, revelations of wonderful intensity, convictions which cannot be reasoned out of existence. My God-given lucidity struck deep into my soul, healing the wounds of my past, as the exquisite splendor, beauty, and peace of Divinity shone into me from the Light. My ego had dissolved into intense, infinite love and it was overwhelming! In that state of non-ego, I was experiencing the supreme gift of Christ-consciousness – the Eternal state of Being. God took away everything I thought I was which left only what He had truly created. Since we are all created out of God, I was able to merge back into Him, as everyone one day will. During this unitive experience I was able to experience what God was experiencing.

Able to observe the physical surroundings below me, my spirit-self floated around the room like a gentle snowflake effortlessly traveling its intended path. The people were seated in their chairs watching me deliver the eulogy. My spirit-self however, was observing them in their non-physical bodies. I was seeing them in their true form as I was. They were all sparks of spiritual Light at the core of their being. Their human bodies were simply a protective covering used to enable the soul to function well in the physical realm. But in the spiritual realm, there is no need for covering of any kind, for the purity of our Being is *Light*.

As I was observing all the people in the audience listening to the eulogy, my love for them poured from the heart of my soul for I realized we are all one. We are all particles of the One who loves all of us without measure.

Moving upward with the Light-God through the chapel ceiling, above the building, the city streets, the state, the country, and the planet, we moved at a tremendous speed into the dark universe. We traveled and stopped to what seemed to me to be the center of the universe. I felt awestruck at the multidimensional cosmos before me. This is probably the hardest part for me to describe because science has not yet discovered or proven what I saw. I saw at least eleven dimensions, unlike a three-dimensional viewing of individual places. It would be more correct for me to describe them as "higher energy spiritual dimensions." It's impossible for me to describe this accurately so you can understand what I am trying to describe. It's like asking me to describe a color to a blind person. I can't, therefore, I must rest with the ineffability of that particular journey.

However, it is my understanding that the new quantum theoretical physicists state that all our knowledge about the absoluteness of our physical reality may be wrong. Quantum physicists in leading universities around the world are seriously investigating what mystics have long suggested that our world is an illusion. The moment I lifted out of my physical body, I realized that I had just left an illusionary reality and had entered into the **real** reality. I had no previous knowledge about quantum physics at that time in my life nor did I ever entertain the idea that we live in an illusionary world. I would have laughed if someone told me this world we live in is an illusion. But that is precisely what I experienced!

Still merged into oneness with the Light-God, we began to travel once again at a tremendous rate of speed going deeper and deeper into the dark universe until we reached the beginning of the creation of the universe. I understood the Light-God as the Supreme and sole Creator of the starting point of everything ever created. To my amazement, I learned that the Light was living energy-the sum total of and infinite energy of the created and uncreated cosmos. Until that very moment, that knowledge had not been part of my belief system. I had always believed our Creator to be a man with a long white robe and long white beard. The Creator that I encountered was an infinite loving Being of Light energy that cannot be conceptualized. It proved to me that humanity has an extremely limited view of who or what the Creator is. However, to help us imagine what the Creator might be, it is reasonable to think of the Creator in a way that makes the Creator's image perceptible and individually meaningful to us.

The Creator showed me that the very first created form emerged from Divine Light as a spark of that same Light, and that all of Creation – everything – from the atoms, molecules, quarks, human beings, has at its core, the spark of Divine Light. This Light is a very pure and perfect form of *Divine energy, or Divine Love.* Its' power is greater than our limited awareness can imagine or comprehend. I also had a vision of seeing humanity in its current evolutionary state of being, symbolized spiritually as being in the caveman era. Just as the cavemen discovered the energy and power of fire and ultimately evolved to a higher state of being, I saw that humanity today has the potential to discover lying within ourselves, the ultimate energy and power of Divine Light and Love. Discovering and utilizing this knowledge would be the catalyst for a new evolutionary world where Heaven on earth will be realized.

That knowledge was a profound insight with which the Light-God was revealing to me. I thought, all we have to do is to *awaken* to the realization of who we are at the core of our being which is Light and Love, and to express that outwardly, unconditionally into the world. That message resonated loud and clear. I understood that was the bottom line. That was humankind's destination.

Once again, I began to feel a sense of rapid movement as the Light and I began to travel back toward earth. As we were nearing the earth, we hovered above our planet stopping to take a closer look at all the social injustices, the wars, the murderers, the chaos. Although this will sound bizarre, I felt there was indeed order to the chaos I was witnessing. Please remember all during my entire experience, I was merged into oneness with the Light-God, having the same loving awareness as God. My ego-self was non-existent, so I wasn't able to judge or perceive anything except Divine unconditional Love. God was love! I was love! Therefore, no other energy other than divine love was in existence.

There appeared only the unfathomable fullness of love beyond space and time. Only love is real. That is what I understood. There were no questions I needed to ask because there was no ego to question anything. God did not have an ego; that is a lower vibrational energy, so how could God judge what "we" were observing with anything less than perfect love? He can't. There is no part to God's character that is less than perfect love. As we viewed mankind's display of loving and unloving behavior on our planet, I understood how sweet and tender was God's love for all of us no matter who we are or what we have done. Our Beloved's pure and sacred love for us is continuous as the stars that shine in the great cosmos. I understood that everything was working out the way it was supposed to work out. Yes, even the worst kind of tragedy.

I cannot articulate this in any way to prevent anyone from regarding this as ludicrous and sheer nonsense. We live in a world in which our egos condition us to respond to negative situations in a negative way. We have not yet learned to live lives of unconditional love. That doesn't mean that we love the behavior if it is bad. It does mean that we can still love the pure, loving *core* of that person's being. The Light of God recognizes the Light of God in others through the rays of Divine-given lucidity that reaches deep within our souls. When our ego attachments have been transcended to the state where we recognize our true connection to our Beloved, then and only then, can we fully begin to understand this Divine Mystery.

A beautiful way of describing this invisible union with God is told by Meister Eckhart.

"The eye by which I see God is the same as the eye by which God sees me. My eye and God's eye are one and the same — one in seeing, one in knowing, and one in loving."

As we began traveling once again at a tremendous rate of speed, the Light and I passed by every person on the face of the earth. I was bursting with unconditional love for everyone, no strings attached, even though I was witnessing some horrific scenes of social upheaval. I understood that each person was playing his/her role, and that it affected the whole. Without that specific part, the whole would be incomplete. Like a picture puzzle, each part was unique and integral, and an important aspect. Missing, the entire picture puzzle would then be disrupted. There was underlying spiritual good to be found in all things.

During this portion of my encounter with the Holy Light, I began to focus upon an intense revelation that was being revealed to me. I began to understand the meaning of unconditional love. In spite of all the chaos on the earth, our Beloved loved everyone equally. I absolutely understood that each person is intimately cherished beyond human comprehension – sinners and saints. My own consciousness was devoid of all ego boundaries. In that state of blissful unity with the Light, I felt ecstatic with the knowledge that I was viewing the earth and its inhabitants from my true self, my soul. Words can never express the mystery of Divine unconditional love, and the soul's unitive consciousness with the Infinite Being. It can never be described; it can only be experienced.

After experiencing the unconditional love for everyone on the planet, the Light-God focused attention on me. In a sanctified embrace of total unconditional Holy Love, I was given a life review. Contrary to what my prior religious beliefs had been of a judgmental God who would decide whether I would go to heaven or hell based on how good or bad a person I was, I found that I was judging myself. All the while, God was loving me unconditionally. That didn't mean that any sin I committed was overlooked and meant that I got away with it. No way!

You see, life reviews are transparent and iridescent as a soap bubble. Every single moment of one's life is brought before one's soul to review. We come face to face with ourselves and see how we measured up to the measuring stick of **love**. Love is the measure of our lives lived, not the

35

accomplishments, social status, monetary gain or anything else. How much did we **love**? How much did we love when it wasn't the easiest thing to do? How did we treat someone who was handicapped, or obese, or poor? How did we treat someone who mistreated us? Did we offer a hug to someone who was feeling weary? Every moment in our life will flood back to us during our life review with each moment held up to the measuring stick of love.

At one point I was shown an onion to illustrate man's ego nature and how we must remove layers and layers of our ego's image of who we are. It's the mask we wear for the world to see. It's the anger, frustrations, envy, jealousy, judgement, self-criticism and a number of other negative messages coming from our ego. My great Teacher showed me that at the core of that onion was a pearl of sweetness which represented the core of our inner self, the Divine qualities of unconditional love.

During my life review I was flabbergasted to understand that even the simplest acts of kindness that one would overlook as insignificant was a major act of our true spiritual selves. We should never underestimate the significance or size of any situation that enables us to attain this infinite goal. By releasing our heart's feeling, we are releasing the power of our Divine kinship to dispel the spiritual darkness of others wherever we go. Nothing is more important than following the inner Voice of conscience, which is the Voice of our Beloved, and conducting our lives to honor who we truly are.

As my experience continued, I wanted to remain with God forever. I couldn't bear the thought of being separated from this Holy bond with my Beloved. Consciously, I began to think of a way to stay. I knew I had to be free of the physical part of me that was delivering the eulogy, so I briefly considered having a heart attack to gain that release. Don't get me wrong. I have a fantastic, loving family who I love very much! Life has been very good to me, so my considerations weren't because of any depression or anything like that. Try to understand that there is nothing on earth that compares with the love of God – nothing! Not even the love of family can compare to the kind of unconditional love that God has for us. Until you can directly experience this unearthly unconditional love for yourself, then you won't be able to understand what I am trying to explain.

Knowing my thoughts, the Light-God communicated telepathically to me, the words,

"No, you cannot stay. I have work for you on earth. You are to become a communicator, to help people understand that there is life after death. Help them become aware of their true nature, and help them to learn to live their lives expressing unconditional love for one another."

My heart was racing to accept this calling because that would be my gift of love to God for the gift of grace I was receiving. Yes, yes, I will do anything I am being asked to do.

God "told" me something else.

"Slow down my child, before you decide to accept this calling, you need to know what you will be getting yourself into. I'm going to show you the negative and the positive aspects of the work I am calling you to do for me."

Suddenly in a flash forward life preview, I saw myself standing before audiences speaking of what I experienced with the Light-God. People were ridiculing me, laughing, shaking their heads in disbelief, and walking out of my pre-sentations. I also saw my entire circle of friends no longer wanting to be my friends because they felt I had changed and was either crazy or fanatical. I saw how upset my father would become when I talked how I had been with God. Those negative previews of my life made me sad. I wasn't sad because people thought I was crazy or fanatical. I wasn't interested in calling attention to myself. I knew in my soul that the ego must not be center stage when one is called to serve the Beloved. I was sad because people did not want to believe the message that came from the Light-God. I knew how much the Light-God loved all His children without measure. God wanted everyone to know about that love through the message that I was being sent back to deliver, and they chose to turn away.

In another flash forward life preview scene, I was shown the positive aspects of the work God was calling me to do for Him. Once again, I saw myself standing before audiences delivering the knowledge I was given to share with others. This time people were listening intently, deeply touched by my sincerity. I saw little red hearts being lifted from their bodies, upwards toward the Creator's Heart for intimacy and renewal. I understood that human consciousness was becoming more elevated to Divine Consciousness and self-realization.

My answer to God's call was a definite yes! I would promise to serve God in this manner until I drew my final breath no matter what obstacles I had to face along the way.

When I gave my answer of acceptance for this calling, I immediately felt a tremendous infusion of knowledge as if volumes and volumes of material from the beginning of time until the end of time entered my consciousness. I have noticed that when I am actually doing the work for God such as writing books or giving talks, the wisdom surfaces.

Telepathically, the Light-God spoke to me and said,

"With the gift you have now received, go forth and tell the masses that life after death exists. You shall all experience my profound love!" That word was emphasized as the message I was to promulgate in my work for God. *"Love is the key to the universe. You must all learn to live in peace and harmony with one another on earth while you have the chance. This will be a very difficult task for you my child, but you shall do it. You are loved!"*

Confidence in my ability to fulfill the calling I was given came when the Light-God said,

"As long as you hold onto my Hand and don't let go, I shall lead and you shall follow. I will prepare the path ahead for you."

The next thing that happened was something remarkable. A scene appeared before me in which I was standing at the head of a very long thick oak wooden table. Seated around the table were twelve individuals who were all dressed in apparel reminiscent of a time period where men wore robe-like garments like the monks wore. All except the three seated to my right next to me had their robe hoods pulled over their heads so I could not see their faces. The three men seated next to me had their faces exposed to me. I never knew those individuals here on earth. The purpose of that gathering of the twelve individuals with me was to help me fulfill the calling that the Light-God willed for me when I returned to earthly physical consciousness.

Deeply humbled for their assistance, I thanked God for their willingness to be of help to me. How that would evolve, I did not know. I simply knew they would help me to fulfill my destiny.

A few years after my experience, I met those three men who were seated at the large wooden table with me whose faces were not covered with their robed hoods. They each lived in different states. I was shocked when I met them because I instantly recognized them from my experience. Since I had never met them previously during my earthly life, you can imagine the surprise I felt when that part of my experience was confirmed in the physical reality. How can this happen?

There is no time on the other side. Everything can happen simultaneously and the soul can see into the past or the future. A soul living in the physical reality can also look past the veil and into the other world of spirit simultaneously just as I did during my unitive experience. My understanding is that the twelve individuals were not allowed to recall their otherworldly experience with me. This would allow those individuals to carry out their part in my "mission" without their human egos interfering, thus preventing them from fulfilling their part in my spiritual work. I am puzzled however, as to why they were all dressed in monk's apparel.

I did not tell those three individuals I recognized as having been on the other side of the veil with me, or that they promised to help me with my calling. If I told them, I did not want them to feel any responsibility to help me. I knew their souls knew what they were meant to do, and I would leave it up to their souls to manifest whatever help they were voluntarily willing to offer me. They did help me enormously, and because of the gratitude I had for them, I decided to tell them about my unitive experience and their role in it after many years had passed. I wanted to express my gratitude to them.

Each person told me they sensed a deep desire to help me, to support me, guide me, and lead me, and opening doors for me. As I said before, their souls knew what they were meant to do, and intuitively, their hearts were led to offer the kind of help I needed to further my work for the Light-God. As if they were walking in the footsteps of God, each person appeared in my life and embraced me with their Light of love.

What about the other nine individuals? Have they appeared in my life as well? As I said before, everyone had their hoods covering their faces except the three seated to my right so I did not know who they were. There have been individuals however, who have appeared in my life to assist me in very big ways. I have a hunch that they are some of those nine unidentified individuals seated at the wooden table. I am very grateful for the love and help those beautiful souls have also given me! I pray for them all the time.

Then with one final, powerful, yet gentle embrace, the Light-God and I *hugged* and the Light began to recede and fade into the distance. Words cannot describe the agonizing longing I felt in wanting to go with God, but I knew the separation was only temporary. One day I would be reunited with God in that home of all homes that was slowly disappearing before my spiritual eyes.

One final word was spoken to me by God. "Books." Placed deep within the heart of my soul, was the understanding that I was to write books and communicate to the masses everything that my Great Teacher taught me while

I was in God's Presence. The written words would become the instrument to bring God's wisdom and Love for all those individuals who have the "eyes to see and the ears to hear" God's loving voice within their own souls.

Like a distant star glimmering steadily in the darkness, the Light faded softly until it was no more. I was left standing at the podium, finishing the eulogy and feeling as if my soul were a thousand tears falling like softly pattering wings of the angels, waking me to the beginning of a great adventurous journey that would last forever. The mystery of what had just happened to me turned into an ecstasy which suddenly overwhelmed my mind like unexpected and exquisite thoughts. Although my thoughts were buzzing like a swarm of bees, I knew I had to maintain my composure while everyone was leaving the funeral home to travel to the cemetery.

Once in the car with my husband and two sons, I blurted out, *"When I was delivering the eulogy, I saw God! I saw John!"*

By the look on their faces, I immediately knew I couldn't say another word to them about what happened to me while delivering the eulogy. My sons looked scared, and my husband looked at me as if he wanted to drive me to the psychiatric hospital instead of going to the cemetery. Fortunately, we drove to the cemetery for John's interment.

My life would never be the same again the moment my unitive experience ended. The embers of my unitive experience lasted days, weeks, months, declining in years, but not forgotten – never forgotten! When I first returned from my unitive experience to physical awareness with my spirit-self back in my physical body, it seemed my soul was hyper attuned to witnessing and feeling more alive and aware of my surroundings than prior to my experience. Everywhere I looked, I loved. Every voice I heard, whether human or not, was like an angel's voice singing its song to me. Every moment felt as if it were like a world of sunshine.

For months, I felt as if I were actually walking six inches above the ground. Even when I walked on the grass, I could feel the blades of grass stretching toward the sun in their individual displays of life. I did not want to crush them beneath my feet. It sounds odd, but I silently apologized for harming even one blade of grass when my feet stepped on them. I was in love with everyone and everything.

This experience not only had implications for my own life, and my relationship with God, but to the everyday world. My previous life broke up, like some great river's ice at the touch of spring. Gone were the many false beliefs about my unworthiness of God's Love. Gone was my low self-esteem. Replaced was a true love of self, not as an egotistical, narcissist type love, but a love that was born of the Sacred Light-God indwelling within me. Gone was the belief that God resided only in a church and faraway up in heaven.

A certainty as no other, the fact was made known to me that God resides within each soul within the physical body, always present, believer or atheist. It became much easier to love everyone, and to extend forgiveness to those who harmed me in any way. In other words, although it had been natural for me to live previously on the surface of my being, now I live in the center of my being, where the Divine Presence within lives who always keeps nudging me to express that Divine Presence in all I do.

For me, my Beloved has been that voice in the wilderness, ever calling me to continued union with Him. I try my best to be faultless and live in the unitive state, but I haven't arrived there yet. True, I arrived at the unitive stage, but not the unitive *state*, or living from the permanent state of

Christ Consciousness where all my thoughts and actions are Christ-like. I do honestly admit however, I do live a pretty good moral and ethical life, but I'm not perfect. I continue to live and breathe the love I have for my Beloved wanting nothing more than to merge into God's Will as my own will.

I still have to square off my life and purge the iniquities of my heart and totally set aside my earthly concerns so that at last my Beloved is my all in all. It is like a baby who cries, and when its mother embraces it and allows him to lie down on her breast. Hearing her heartbeat, he settles down and begins his deep slumber, at peace and comforted.

Such is my heart and soul when I feel those moments when my Beloved is nearer to me than my heartbeat. I fall to my knees only wanting to do the will of God as my own. But I know that I am weak and cannot do it on my own. I need my Beloved to walk with me, talk with me, and work through me when times are good and when they are tough. Every moment the mystery of life with Him is like an angel's kiss.

I have come to understand that everything that happens in my life is exactly what has been needed. Such an outlook towards my circumstances and faith in my relationship with God has made me content with everything. I have no desire in my life except the desire to reach passionately after Him, to always dwell with Him, and to serve in ways that honor Him.

The female saint Rabi's al-Adawiyya said:
"I have two ways of loving You:
A selfish one
And another way that is worthy of You.
In my selfish love, I remember You and You alone.

In that other love, You lift the veil
And let me feast my eyes on Your Living Face."

Sumnun the Lover speaks what my heart speaks:
    "I have separated my heart from this world –
    My heart and Thou are not separate.
    And when slumber closes my eyes,
    I find Thee between the eye and the lid."

CHAPTER 4
EVELYN UNDERHILL

"The spiritual life is part of every man's life, and until he has realized it he is not a complete human being."
— Evelyn Underhill

Evelyn Underhill is best known for her book *Mysticism: A Study in the Nature and Development of Man's Spiritual Consciousness*. The book is deemed the classic book on mysticism. Through her study of the mystics and even more through her own experiences, Underhill emphasized that *"mysticism is the art of union with Reality"* and *"a mystic is a person who has attained that union in a greater or less degree; or who aims at and believes in such attainment."*

The goal is union with God, or the unitive life, where one's life is solely infused by God's life and love. Mysticism is the bridge that connects man to God, and brings God's Wisdom and Love to man. It is through knowledge, loving action, and dedicating one's life to the mystical path that one is able to realize the inner union with God.

In her book, Mysticism, Underhill writes what she considers to be the characteristic stages or experiences that mark the progress of the mystic. I will also be supplementing this knowledge with the knowledge I received during my unitive experience with the Light-God as it pertains to this mystical path of spiritual development. When I entered into the unitive reality, the highest realm of consciousness – one with God, I was granted total knowledge as if I were re-membering wisdom from a faraway past as well as revealing all knowledge in the distant future. The spiritual wisdom I received was meant to be shared with humanity in order that all may realize we were all created for the spiritual journey toward union with God. My deepest desire is that the books I write and the wisdom I share will reveal a depth of God many have not previously known, or perhaps even imagined. The mystical path will help one to realize that deeper state of knowing.

THE AWAKENING STAGE

The *awakening stage* is the first stage when the person starts to become aware that their personal-self experiences the presence of light, a spiritual vision, or a sense of cosmic connectedness. The individual begins to become aware of the presence of something supernatural, a feeling in which everything is connected to everything. Underhill claims *"this experience usually is abrupt and well-marked, and is ac-companied by intense feelings of joy and exhaltation."*

Generally speaking, most near-death experiencers awakened to this first stage in the mystical journey toward the unitive experience and a return to Source. Their hearts have been filled with joy and love unspeakable, sometimes comprehending the nature of reality, or other aspects of wisdom. The common denominator of many near-death experiences is a feeling that consciousness has expanded beyond the usual ego boundaries and has transcended the limitations of time and space. What is perceived is said to come from another world, or at least another dimension and is central in mystical experiences.

Once a near-death experiencer has been awakened, there is hard work living with the spiritual guidance obtained during our near-death experiences. PMH Atwater, noted NDE researcher found after studying thousands of near-death experiencers, claims that it takes about seven years to adjust and integrate the near-death experience into our lives. It takes time, patience, commitment and courage to bridge the world of matter and spirit and to live in accordance with the ideals we experienced. Even though we were catapulted into a higher state of consciousness than prior to our NDE, we haven't fully realized divinity. We have a long way to go before graduating from our still limited awareness of ultimate consciousness.

If we are to flower with awakening to higher states of consciousness, we must truly have a genuine desire for it and liberation from everything that is false in us. Awakening to our true nature is no easy task. The preparation calls for a change in consciousness whereby one is able to see the underlying unity of all things. No matter how hard a person tries to achieve awakening, it can never be achieved – only discovered.

My personal awakening stage came when I was a four-year-old child. I attended a Ukrainian Catholic Church where my grandparents worshipped as Ukrainian immigrants. Because most of the congregation were Ukrainian and couldn't speak English very well, the priest spoke the entire two hour service in Ukrainian. No English words were spoken. You can imagine how boring that must have been for such a small child. I hated going to church but mother insisted we go every Sunday. I had no choice in the matter.

I still remember that day as if it were yesterday. One particular Sunday church service I suddenly became unaware of the priest, the altar boys, the congregation, and even my mother seated next to me. Somehow I felt my spirit-self being lifted into a misty, fog-like place where my friend, God was. No, I didn't "see" God; I felt His Presence with me and I was extremely happy! Oh my goodness, how I talked His ear off, chattering about everything I did that week – helping mother around the house, walking to grandmom's house through the woods, spotting a turtle in a small puddle of muddy water and poking it to crawl out of the water and onto dry land. On and on I chattered until mother's arms nudged me and told me it was time to go home; church service was over. Two hours had passed without my awareness of anything transpiring during the church service. I was with God that entire time.

In my thoughts, I said, *"I have to go now God, but I love you very much. Thanks for listening to me."* Then clearly, I heard a masculine voice in my head saying, *"I love you also my child."*

From that moment on, my spirituality blossomed big-time! I couldn't wait to go to church every Sunday, hoping that I would sit next to my friend God again in that foggy, misty place, but it wasn't to be. Nevertheless, I felt contented just being seated in church every Sunday, quietly, *knowing* that my friend God was seated right next to me even though I could not see Him. I continued to "talk" to him in my silent thoughts every time I went to church and I developed a very close bond with Him that lasted throughout my life.

On my daily walks to my grandmother's house, about

three miles away, I always stopped at a Catholic Church on the way to pray in their outdoor grotto. It was so beautiful. I always prayed on the kneeling pad in front of the statue of the Blessed Virgin Mary. There were lit candles flickering in the warm sunlight. Throughout the grotto were colorful flowers whose aroma filled my senses with such sweet joy. I imagined that my friend God was kneeling beside me. **Oh, how I loved God!**

Although the initial seed experience of my spiritual development was a spontaneous mystical experience with God, I cultivated that seed with constant conscious cultivation, not knowing that one day I would be given the gift of the unitive experience. There was no ulterior motive for me to seek anything from God through the years of my spiritual development. There was only an inner longing that I had to experience the loving bond I had with my friend, God.

I absolutely knew from that first moment of my childhood mystical experience, that God was always with me and would never leave me. What joy I felt! Just to be present in the silence of my daily prayers, or sitting on the green grass on a warm sunny day thinking about how much I loved loved God was the feeling of, "Ahhh."

I spent many years bringing fresh flowers during the month of May that I placed on an altar I created in my bedroom since early childhood until I married. It was my small gift to my Beloved while kneeling for an hour just being available and receptive to the inflowing and out-flowing of our love for one another. Those moments spent with my friend God were heavenly, and in the truest sense, they were Divine.

In retrospect, knowing God as I did without knowing "about" God, was my path toward experiencing my eventual unitive experience. It was a long journey from age four to age thirty-eight, a journey with all types of twists and turns, ups and downs. I had developed an intimacy with my Beloved without having been schooled in any religious teachings. My teaching was direct experience rather than scholarly knowledge.

I could give you a thousand examples of how my young spiritual life blossomed, carrying me into adulthood, but I suppose, that's for another book. Yikes! Let's continue now with Underhill's example of the second stage of mysticism called *Purgation*.

THE PURGATION STAGE

The Purgation stage is marked by the individual's recognition of his or her imperfections that stand in the way of coming into deeper contact with the Transcendent and tries to compensate for them with self-discipline. The path is letting go of all that is not love to create a space in one's life for that which is love.

Evelyn Underhill writes in *Mysticism*, *"no mystic can omit the initial stage of purgation and a putting aside of the old for the new to be born."*

We must begin to become more aware of those parts of our nature that impedes our progress toward becoming the person God had intended us to be. If we are willing to change the thoughts about every situation that has held us victim for so long, we can then change the actions we take. Real change is made real by our thoughts first. If we stumble along the way, no problem. As long as we are genuinely seeking to grow spiritually, our constant companion and friend, God, will help us. We are never alone on this journey.

I was not a "seeker." I had no knowledge about mysticism

until I began writing this book when I researched mysticism in the literature. All my spiritual experiences were sudden and without me doing anything consciously to receive them. However, I now feel in retrospect, that my soul had been preparing me all along to develop unknowingly, the ability to respond and heed my inner response to God's call.

My moral and ethical compass had always been very high since my awakening experience as a child. I was devoted to God, always feeling the magnetic pull of His Loving Presence within me. I actually wanted to become a nun and dedicate my life to serving God, but I decided against that when I reached puberty and discovered boys. I truly believe that this deep love I felt for God ever since being a small child was instrumental in developing my spirituality so that one day, God would grant me by His grace, the gift of the unitive oneness experience with Him. I never once gave up my love for my best friend, God, even though, as you will soon learn, my relationship with Him would utterly perish, like a blown-out flame.

Saint John of the Cross said it best:

"What prepares the soul to be united with God is the desire for God."

THE ILLUMINATION STAGE

The third stage that Underhill describes is the *illumination* stage. A mystical experience characterizes this stage. The ego has been subdued enough that an actual experience such as a near-death experience people have is able to occur. The ego has always prevented that from happening making the person feel separate from everything as we all do. Those in this stage have made progress and have their passions and worldly desires better under control. With the ego better under control, Reality is able to slip in. Whether it's for a moment or an hour, everything has changed. The take away is that once the experience is felt, there is no turning back. One begins to discover by Grace, (not our own efforts) God's Love really does flow through us. That Divine Love reveals Itself by our capacity to truly love others, not only our immediate loved ones, but even our enemies. The mind becomes more enlightened to spiritual things and the practice of virtue, but those desires may still get in the way of a deeper experiential union with God.

The soul seeks progress in the spiritual life and in all the virtues with an effort to let go of everything that is not love, but purgation is still somewhat incomplete. One isn't perfect when one reaches the illumination stage; it is an indication of where one is in their spiritual growth. The individual should continue their purification on deeper and deeper levels, not having to give up things, just their attachment to them. People need to realize that there is a path to follow as with awakening. If the work for the illumination experience is not done, there will be no corresponding growth.

Understanding the various paths toward higher consciousness is helpful for the individual to be able to discern one's highest goal and asking their inner guidance for help to be led in the direction for their next step on their spiritual growth path. Rather than being lost in confusion and emotional misery, it is important to maintain one's purity of consciousness and keep their spiritual goal on the right path. Help will always be available to the genuine seeker. Quite unexpectedly, one will be led to the right material, people or events that is important for the focus of their spiritual life.

However, the spiritual work is not yet completed in the illumination stage before one is able to reach the highest stage of spiritual maturity, direct experiential union with God. For most, the illumination stage in the mystical journey ends.

This earth school has many ups and downs, fears, frustrations, anger, illness – you name it. I have become okay with seeing everything as opportunities for still more growth that I need to personally work on. But there have been moments in my life where my spirit has taken me to great heights, when I was able to recognize that life doesn't have to crush me. The quiet voice that always speaks the truth helps to lift my eyes above the struggle to remember that in all moments, Spirit is calling me to be who I truly am, God's child.

On a chilly March evening in 1989, our house burned to the ground. Our family was in the house at the time, unaware that the fire had started in the garage. Lucky for us, a neighbor who lived one-quarter of a mile down the road happened to see smoke coming out of our roof. The man phoned us and asked if we were burning our wood burning stove. No, we weren't. That phone call alerted all of us to the immediate danger taking place. Within seconds, thick black smoke began to infiltrate the entire house and we couldn't breathe. Fortunately, we knew to drop to our knees and crawl on the floor where there was a pocket of clean air for us to breathe. There was no time to be afraid; only time to crawl to the front door and escape out to safety outdoors. Had we not known there was clean air below the deadly thick black smoke, we wouldn't be alive today.

Once safely outside, we heard explosions taking place within the house as we stood on the front lawn watching everything we worked hard for so many years collapsing as if it were a pricked balloon.

Because we didn't live in a housing development or have

city water, a neighbor called the voluntary fire department fifteen miles away in the country to come to our aid. It took them one half hour to arrive, and when they came, they came without any water in their tanks! We live right across the street from a large pond that was designated for fire use only, so I told the fire chief that he could gain access to the water from the pond. He looked at the pond and refused to siphon any water into his tanks because of the algae and debris in the pond, which meant he had to call in another fire department for assistance. The house was gone by that time.

An undefined sadness seemed to have fallen over my husband and our sons, settling down on their minds like a shadow. What would we do now? Everything is gone! A voice in my head spoke soft and sweet, *"Do not fear, I am here."* When I heard that voice, I knew that I was going to be okay – really okay.

Many friends and strangers came to our aid, offering us a place to stay and giving us items of necessity until we could get to a store to purchase them ourselves. A local men's church group helped us clean up the mess and oh, what a mess there was! But everyone pitched in to help us. Because we were underinsured, we had to do most of the rebuilding work ourselves. I went to garage sales every weekend to purchase items for the house that we didn't have the money to spend on new things. Working to rebuild our home was a lot of work, but we were able to get it done and move back into our new house on Christmas Eve, 1989.

When many people heard about the fire, they were all saying the same thing. *"You must have been so scared."* No, I wasn't. Others said, *"You must be so devastated."* No, I wasn't. Others said, *"You lost everything that was precious to you, you must feel as if you can't go on."* No I didn't feel like that.

Others were trying to imagine how they would have felt had they gone through that experience, and they couldn't understand why I wasn't feeling upset about losing everything.

But honestly, I did not feel attached to the things we lost. Our family was safe, and our love for each other pulled us through the difficult days ahead of rebuilding our lives. Looking back, I am certain that the still small voice I heard in my mind that night reassuring me that I would be okay and our so-called disaster presented me with another opportunity to detach from the things of this world and rely on my spirit to guide me the rest of the way, along the mystical path I am on. To this day, I have never longed for anything we loved and lost in the fire. Our family survived. That is all that mattered.

DARK NIGHT OF THE SOUL

The fourth stage is what Saint John of the Cross called the *Dark Night of the Soul,* a preparation to enter the unitive way. This is a time of trial where it feels as if God no longer loves the seeker. The soul plunges into a deep abyss of darkness and nothingness. It is often described as a dark cloud descending upon the person the moment it happens. The only cause of Dark Night is that God intercedes and removes the ego. This is the defining characteristic of Dark Night. Up to that point for his entire life, the mystic, and all of us, relate to God, the world, and each other through the ego. Now the person is without an ego for the first time in his entire life. So obviously, he is unable to relate to anything, including God, and he thinks God has abandoned him. This causes anxiety, depression and fear. He eventually sinks to the bottom of these emotions. Some say they feel like they are in an abyss. Then, through the Grace of God, he finds God at the rock bottom of the abyss and finds that he relates to God on a new level in exactly the same way as Christ did.

Now for the rest of his life he EXPERIENCES God as one with him and not in a dual relationship as the rest of us do. This exact moment ends the Dark Night and begins the Unitive State. He is "constantly aware of God being aware of him."

The concept of the Dark Night has come to be confused with depression. They are however, not entirely separate things. Clinical depression is a sad event caused by events such as the loss of a loved one, a serious illness, or a biochemical problem. The person is unable to go about the normal business of their life. They may contemplate suicide and or self-loathing. On the other hand, those who experience the Dark Night although challenging, are able to function well and remain quite active.

When depression ends, not much changes in one's life. Beliefs and habits remain unchanged. However, when the dark night ends, everything in life changes and life is beautiful again. One's beliefs, perceptions, and meaning in life are now better understood.

The Dark Night is purely an act of God. It is God preparing one's soul for a spiritual transformation to draw one closer to Him. The soul then breaks through the Dark Night and has *experiential* knowledge of God, closer to Him than they are to themselves, closer than the air that is breathed. This break-through experience of the Dark Night prepares us so that our wills and hearts move in perfect harmony with God's.

I don't believe I went through the Dark Night, but I certainly went through a sixteen-year period of my life in which I believed with my entire being that God no longer loved me.

I already mentioned that my deep abiding love for God was ever present within my heart ever since childhood. My love went deeper than simply believing in a loving God. The nearness I always felt at the center of my being was my friend, God who had taken up residence within the heart of that small child and who never left me.

What then, changed? I fell in love with my very first boyfriend and the first boy I ever kissed. We met and fell in love while dancing at a high school dance. We married and were together for over fifty years until his death.

As is the custom in the Catholic Church, all those preparing for marriage must meet with the priest for pre-marital counseling. Ched and I went together to meet with the priest to discuss all the details of our impending marriage. After all introductions were made and all the cordial conversation took place, the priest reached into his desk drawer and pulled out a sheet of paper and asked both Ched and me to sign it.

"What's this?" Ched asked the priest.

"It's the document you need to sign that states both of you promise to raise any and all children that you may have as Catholic. It's our church law." He replied.

"No way," declared Ched. *"I won't sign this. I believe in letting the children decide for themselves what religion they want to be."*

I could feel all the tension in my body well up like steel, my heart beating faster and faster. My fingers were knotted like a cord. Ched couldn't hear my silent words screaming, *"Just sign the paper – sign! We could let the children decide what religion they want to honor when they are old enough."*

Ched continued explaining how he didn't want to take

away his children's right to decide what they wanted to believe.

Looking straight into Ched's eyes, the priest asked Ched, *"Do you believe in God?"* Very calmly, Ched answered, "no."

Then, just as I dreaded, the priest turned to me and asked, *"Did you know that Ched feels this way?"* Meekly, I replied, *"Yes."*

"I'm sorry, but I cannot marry you in the sanctuary, he replied. The sanctuary is not for atheists. I can marry you in my office, but not in the sanctuary."

The priest's demeanor took on a rather cold as stone attitude towards us, unlike the gracious and kind introductions when we first met him. Turning to me he said, *"and you young lady, I want to meet with you privately in my office Thursday night at seven o'clock."*

Ched and I left the priest's office that night each lost in our own thoughts. We were not expecting to be treated so harshly by a priest. We weren't sure what we wanted to do.

I decided that I would meet with the priest privately at seven o'clock the following Thursday night. I sat down in his office quaking like a jelly fish, feeling scared. After all, I was taught that priests are God's messengers and anything a priest said was truthful. His demeanor towards us was very unpleasant, so I figured I was going to be in for a rough session with him.

It didn't take the priest very long to scold me for wanting to marry an atheist. I was so in love with Ched and I wanted to let the priest know that Ched was the perfect marriage partner for me. Even if he was an atheist, he was an honorable person. Noticing the priest's white collar pressing tightly against his throat, his face turning beet red, my heart suddenly felt like it wasn't capable of beating any longer.

How was I going to convince the priest that Ched was

the love of my life and I wanted to marry this person? How was the priest going to convince me that I was going to go to Hell if I married an atheist?

We spent the next two hours arguing our positions. The priest's position was that I was a horrible sinner and my position was that if I was such a bad sinner, God would forgive me if I repented and asked for forgiveness. After all, God and I were bonded like super glue together in our love for one another. Surely, I would be able to convince the priest that I was a good person.

I was not gaining ground with the priest. At one point the priest said, *"It is your responsibility as a Catholic to convert Ched to Christianity, and specifically to Catholicism. Because you have failed to do this, you are an unworthy Catholic. God is watching over you and sees that you are not converting Ched. God is disgusted with you!"*

The priest's words pierced my heart like an arrow. All the blood must have been draining from my face, but I managed not to cry. My Beloved was angry with me! No, I couldn't bear that. No words were forming in my throat to rebut what the priest was telling me. I just sat there absorbing the harsh words the priest said to me as if in shock.

"Young lady, I want to continue these sessions with you three times a week for two hours a session." He said sternly. I agreed, silently hoping for resolution of this important matter.

For the next four weeks my sessions with the priest continued three times a week. Why, you may ask, did I want to return and deal with that kind of talk coming from the priest? I was young at the time. I was raised not to think for myself with regard to matters of my religion. I was a sheep, I admit.

Each time I sat down in my chair looking at the priest seated behind his thick desk, I was prepared to state my love for Ched, my love for God, and that I was a good person. I was not the person the priest portrayed me as being. Every time I tried to make my point, the priest would interrupt me with cutting words, *"You are the scum of the earth. God cannot forgive your sin. God can forgive a murderer, but not you. Don't even pray to God anymore because God doesn't want to listen to you. Don't go to church anymore either because you are not worthy to step inside God's clean white sanctuary. You are filthy and you are not fit to be in God's presence. If you do, you will feel the wrath of God upon you!"*

Wow! His words pierced deep into my soul. At the end of the month I was spiritually shattered. No matter how hard I tried to communicate my deep love for God and God's love for me, the priest was able to tear down my beliefs. What resulted was a loss of my own personal power and self-esteem. I took on as absolute truth, the priest's perceptions, and I discarded my own. I was left spiritually naked. There was no room in my heart for a speck of hope that God would still love me. If God could not love me, I could not love myself. I felt like raw sewage and the worst human being on the face of the earth.

Let me remind you, back in those days, and I'm talking in the 40's and 50's, it was common for the Catholics in my congregation to hold priests in high esteem. They could do no wrong. Because I believed they were divinely inspired, their words were truthful because their words were entrusted to them by God in order to guide the flock.

At that time in my spiritual life, I believed in a judgmental God who keeps score of our good and bad deeds who would send us either to heaven or hell depending on how good or bad a life we lived. In my case, I was certain I would be going to hell at the end of my life and there was nothing I could do about it. God no longer loved me, so I was told, and I believed that with every fiber of my being. There was no sense in even trying to hope that God could forgive me for wanting to marry the love of my life, an atheist and failing to convert him to Catholicism.

Ched and I decided to get married in his family's Presbyterian Church. The day I walked down the aisle holding my father's arm, I silently cried. This was supposed to be the happiest day of my life, but that's not how I felt. Slowly approaching the altar where the minister was waiting for me to arrive, I looked at the altar and the cross and I felt ugly, like trash. How dare I approach the sacred altar with my deplorable presence? I tried not to look at the sacred images, instead focusing my eyes on Ched instead.

For the next sixteen years, I had no relationship with God. I missed my best friend God, but felt I didn't deserve to be loved by Him. Several times I started to pray and ask forgiveness for the "grave sin" I had been told by the priest I had committed, but I couldn't pray because I reminded myself that God no longer wanted to have a relationship with me. I was rotten to the core. Why would God want to hear the aching words of my heart? Hopelessness set in.

One time I decided that in order to be forgiven for my "sin," I would have to attend a church service where I believed God to live. At that time in my life, that's where I believed God lived. I had no idea God lived inside of us. God lived far away in heaven, and also, only in the Catholic Church. That is what I believed.

One Sunday morning, I got my courage up to attend a Catholic Church with just a shred of hope that my Beloved would welcome me back to His loving arms. It took a great deal of faith to actually drive to that church, walk inside and take a seat in the pew. My eyes began to scan everything sacred, reminding me of so many years I had not seen the inside of a church. Without warning, I suddenly began to feel sick to my stomach. The words of the priest so many years earlier flooded my mind, reminding me that I was not supposed to be sitting in church with so many "good" people.

"Don't go to church anymore," I remember him saying to me so many years earlier. *"You are not worthy to be in the presence of God's clean sanctuary. You are filth in His eyes. If you do go to church, you will feel the wrath of God come upon you."*

The priest's words kept ringing in my mind like the tolling of a bell, over and over again, reminding me I was utter scum.

The haunting memory of those words he spoke to me intensified my conviction that I was trespassing upon sacred grounds. His words churned over and over in my mind until I couldn't take it any longer. I felt nauseated. I began to shake. The contempt I felt for myself was so strong that I convinced myself that the priest told me the truth about myself. The horrible feelings that surfaced while sitting in the pew were indicative that I was actually feeling the "wrath of God," or so I believed.

I couldn't stay there any longer. I had to remove my despicable presence from our Creator's clean white sanctuary. Once outdoors, I vomited. That experience convinced me there was not a molecule of hope that my Beloved would love me again. From that moment on, I vowed I would never attempt under any circumstance to rebuild my relationship with God.

As devastating as those sixteen years were living without a relationship with my Beloved, **I never stopped loving God deeply.** I can't even recall harboring any negative feelings toward the priest or with God. The only true anger, resentment, and blame I felt lay squarely upon my own self, which in retrospect, was not warranted.

The priest was a good person, only looking out for my greatest good, the salvation of my soul. As a priest, that was his responsibility, and he did the best he knew at the time. Unfortunately, he chose fear to motivate me, as many at that time did, preaching hellfire and damnation. That caused a fear reaction in me, which is the opposite of love, and which I would learn later, is not of God.

This may not have been a dark night of the soul, but I do believe that period in my life had some important role in playing in the eventual and abrupt touches of God's Love that my soul perhaps, was rewarded for, culminating with the blessing of the unitive experience later in my life. I would like to think that for those sixteen years that I truly believed God no longer loved me and I believed I was doomed for hell at the end of my life, **God saw that I still loved Him immensely and unconditionally.**

"My God, Thou knowest that I have ever desired to love thee alone. It has been my only ambition."

– Therese of Lisieux

UNITIVE STAGE

The fifth stage that Underhill describes is the unitive stage, the highest and final stage of the mystical journey. This is the exact same consciousness that Christ was BORN into. He did not have to achieve it. And it's the same consciousness that the entire world will eventually have, (Thy Kingdome come, Thy Will be done, on EARTH as it is in heaven.) In other words we are praying for the world to be enlightened as God ultimately intends it to be. At last the soul is transformed in God. The usual sense of self as a separate, isolated individual is dissolved. The soul has been taken by the very special grace of God, *into God* where one's ego is non-existent. There, in the splendor of the Holy God, the soul and God are One. There exists not a simply external relationship, but a mystical *union* of God and the soul of man. In Unitive, the mystic gives up free will so that his will is in *union with God's Will.*

Saint John of the Cross who had a unitive experience said:

"In thus allowing God to work in it, the soul...is at once illumined and transformed in God, and God communicates to it His supernatural Being, in such wise that it appears to be God Himself, and has all that God Himself has. And this union comes to pass when God grants the soul this supernatural favour, that all the things of God and the soul are one in participant transformation; and the soul seems to be God rather than a soul, and is indeed God by participation; although it is true that its natural being, though thus transformed, is as distinct from the Being of God as it was before."

Those who had the unitive experience as far as I could find in my research were Jesus, St. John of the Cross, Teresa of Avila, St Francis, St. Paul, and the Christian mystic and former nun, Bernadette Roberts. All the apostles were in the unitive state after Pentecost. It is a very, very rare experience.

Saint Teresa of Avila spoke of her unitive experience:

"It seemed to me there came the thought of how a sponge absorbs and is saturated with water; so, I thought, was my soul, which was overflowing with that divinity and in a certain way rejoicing within itself and possessing the three Persons. I also heard the words: "Don't try to hold Me within yourself, but try to hold yourself within Me."

Someone can have a direct experience of God without it being a unitive experience. Take for example, this person's account. *"I received a vision from the LORD. In the vision, I was standing in our back yard and suddenly the entire area was illuminated and the appearance of our yard looked so beautiful. I sensed the LORD's Presence and I immediately ran towards the LORD and I hugged Him. After that the LORD walked a distance from me and said, "Come follow me" and I charged towards the LORD and the vision ended."*

Remember, the only qualifier for a unitive experience is that only God is present and there is no "self" witnessing the experience. When both the experiencer and God are present as in the above example, it is an illumination mystical experience, not a unitive experience. **Union** with God! That is the unitive experience in a nutshell. It is not blending into the ocean, the cosmos, everyone on the planet but merging **into and seeing from God's vision or understanding.**

Many near-death experiencers describe being in the presence of the Light with both God and the individual. If a near-death experiencer doesn't understand the unitive experience that I am talking about, then the person didn't have a unitive experience. If he had a unitive experience, he'll understand completely what I am saying, and no other explanation will be necessary.

The profound intellect and wise hearts of the mystics and

saints repeatedly tell us that the unitive experience cannot be grasped by concepts and words. I too, found great difficulty in writing about this experience so others can comprehend what I am describing.

"If you can grasp it, then it is not God."
— Saint Augustine

What we can know about God reflects the human *experience* of God, and in the end, that's all we can really know of Him. It is helpful however, to liberate God from limitations of *any* kind from images, ideas, stories, etc. thereby raising the mind to its highest level, to its own Godlike potential and nature.

The unitive state is only achieved by God's grace but it is up to us to get on the path to Him.

Yunus Emre writes:

"There is an I in me,
Deeper than me,
Whose eyes look at me
From inside of me.

CHAPTER 5

MYSTICISM

"The spiritual life is part of every man's life, and until he has realized it he is not a complete human being."
— Evelyn Underhill

For my readers, I hope this book will be an invitation to take your faith to a new and deeper love of intimacy with God. I hope to add to this great body of work so that others may "taste" what the mystical life is all about. I have personally lived this life, and therefore believe that personal accounts add a great dimension to the understanding of the mystical life that we are all called to live.

As the Carmelite writer Ruth Burrows puts it:

"The mystical life is beyond our power, nothing we can do can bring it to us, but God is longing to give it to us, to all of us, not to a select few."

"What does mysticism really mean? It means the way to attain knowledge. It's close to philosophy, except in philosophy you go horizontally while in mysticism you go vertically."
—Elie Wiesel

Mystical experiences have been reported throughout history by people of all races and religions, including Christians, Jews, Muslims, Hindus, Buddhists, Taoists, Zoroastrians, Native Americans, atheists, agnostics, and those who consider themselves "spiritual but not religious."

Mysticism is not a philosophy or opinion. It has nothing to do with the pursuit of paranormal experiences. It involves a disciplined and intense movement towards ever higher levels of reality, and ever deeper identification with the Divine. The aim of the seeker is to draw oneself with one's whole being "homeward," but always under the guidance of the heart.

The goal of the mystic is union with God, or the unitive life, where one's life is solely infused by God's life and love in which all desires are totally fulfilled, and the heart overflows with unconditional love. This love is not the superficial affection or emotion we so often identify with. Rather, it is a total dedication of the will; the deep seated desire of the soul towards its Source. This pure ardent love can never find true satisfaction except in moving the whole self towards the Divine Presence within.

One of the most moving expressions of mystical love is found in the twenty-third chapter of the Gospel of Luke. There, the author conveys that Jesus, in his pain, asked God to forgive his persecutors. Likewise, we find in the mystical heart, that not only do we forgive others, but we forgive ourselves as well.

Mysticism is the bridge that connects man to God, and brings God's Wisdom and Love to man. It is through the pursuit of knowledge, loving action, and dedicating one's life to the mystical path that one is able to realize the inner union with God. It is never self-seeking for some type of personal reward. The mystic obtains satisfaction because he does not seek it.

"Attainment, comes only by means of this sincere, spontaneous, and entire surrender of yourself and all things." Only then will the soul slowly awaken to the beauty of itself and to the beauty of the Divine.

–Dionysius the Areopagite

The spiritual journey toward living the mystical life is discovering and living the Truth of our Being. No one can give it to us. No matter how many books we may read on the subject, or take workshops, attend lectures, Truth can never be achieved – only discovered and given to us by Grace. There must be an actual *experience* of Truth.

The one who experiences transcendence is aware of his humility in becoming a true mystic.

"First you go toward the light, next you're in the light, you are the light."

–Sai Baba

Mystics bring us new knowledge of higher consciousness, but unless one lives that higher consciousness, one cannot be considered a mystic. Jesus' test of higher consciousness still stands:

"By their fruits ye shall know them."

A genuine mystic is not one who simply has a mystical view of the universe. There are some near-death experiencers for instance, who do not go past communicating their mystical experiences in all their splendor, the lovely visions, the celestial music, etc. However, if inner experience is not translated into outer form, the mystical experience is short-circuited. Near-death and other spiritually transformative experiences open doors to higher consciousness and of course, have value. But the most important point to be understood is their value is *not in the experience itself*, but in emptying the egocentric consciousness itself.

We so easily become centered back in the ego-mind, where we find comfort in our self-centered nature. The real danger is of attitude. Pride can lead to spiritual deception, fear can cause one to give up and rationalize away the need to stay on the mystical path.

From Genesis, to the Word of God, the Apostles, the saints, theologians throughout the centuries and today say the same: God made us to be like Him, wants us to become like Him, and will ultimately transform us into being like Him.

"The center of the soul is God."
—St. John of the Cross

Mystics know that we come from a state of oneness with God and with all humanity. The mystical path is the journey we undertake to get back to that. It's about seeing reality the way Jesus did, not by behaving with more morality, but attaining the state of unitive consciousness, one with God.

I cannot speak for all near-death experiencers, certainly that would be a gross mistake. But I do believe that many think their experience is an exceptional one that lets them see God's "special world" apart from this one, and they are correct. They had what is called a mystical experience. They have no idea that for those that have a near-death experience, it is the first baby step in a long journey that we all have to make along the mystical path toward *union* with God.

Most people, some near-death experiencers included, believe that God lives apart from us and has abandoned this world. They wonder where He was during the school shootings. They have no idea that we have free will to do whatever we please and the responsibility that entails. They don't know that we choose to do things to each other and God allows us to do it because of this free will. That's the agreement. They don't see God occupying every atom of this world because they choose not by doing the work involved to close the chasm. Most don't even know anything about this mystical path.

The Catholic Church and I surmise other faiths as well, give the same sermons on the same Sundays of the liturgical year and never talk about this. If you've gone to church for fifty years you've heard the same sermons on their relative Sunday fifty times. You don't really learn anything about what I am speaking of. The mystical path from awakening to illumination through dark night of the soul to the unitive state is the way to close the chasm so one can experience God being totally aware of you and you totally aware of God every second of your existence. He is indeed with us all every second. But many do not know this.

A near-death experience, as wonderful as it is, is only the literal first step toward a much larger picture and not the end in itself. Mysticism is that road map toward the end stage, union with God. Many people told me they want to have an experience like I did. *"How do I have one?"* they ask? My only answer is that you can't have an experience with the hope of having an experience at all; that's ego talking and slows you down or stops you from progressing. The sole motive must be God and nothing else. To humbly and lovingly long for God and God alone – not having any kind of sensational experience – this is the path of awakening.

I see this all the time with people thinking they are pursing God and they are just a slave to their egos wanting experiences and feeling good. You cannot induce a unitive experience at all. It manifests only by Divine Grace.

The more I read about the mystics and saints, I learned that in many instances, they had perhaps years of being prepared for their dramatic moments of ecstasy and revelations, often unknowingly. They had paved the way gradually with perhaps little awakenings before their big moments which can appear at any stage in one's life.

Thomas Aquinas received his mystical awakening three months before he died at the age of fifty. Thomas Merton received his awakening midway through his life in 1958 and died in 1968. Julian of Norwich was only in her thirties when she had her experiences and lived well into her seventies. Surely, God had been touching them in ways so they could recognize the mysterious longing in their souls which would influence them to recognize the call within them, thus setting them on the path toward becoming infused with God's own Holy presence later on in life.

Thomas Aquinas and Thomas Merton had been priests for years, and Julian of Norwich was a devout follower of God seeking greater intimacy with Him. They were people who prayed, who prepared their hearts and souls with an inner longing for God and yielding to the call of the Beloved. Many other mystics and the saints did the same.

The mystical life is not for a select few, because humans are wired for a life lived in and through a mystical connection with the Beloved. Perhaps you have also at some point in your life recognized at least one spiritual awakening no matter how small or humble it may have been. Chances are that you can now look at it in retrospect and see how it may have taken you from one place in your spiritual life to a higher one.

Every living thing is working out a part of the Divine Plan. Human beings are living for a purpose vastly more important than they can conceive. We learn what is within the scope of human knowledge which is only the semblance of reality, but when we perceive wisdom through the soul, we have access to the essence of reality. In order to carry on life in the material world, it is necessary for us to have what I will call, the lesser instrument of the physical body, or the ego.

The average person's ego is aware only of a very limited person, a person whose powers are constricted by matter and inhibited by suffering, misunderstanding and emotion. The soul senses cannot reach the mind unless that mind has learned to open itself up to receive the higher realization brought through to consciousness from soul perception.

The ego is always insistent upon his rights, and it is the driving power that will haggle, fight, and create endless dilemmas from which it must free itself before it can progress. Ego's driving force is fear. It is time for us to understand that we are being called to live in accordance with Divine Intent. However, I must say that fear has created inhibitions, for it is natural that one should feel a certain awe of the unknown when treading on a path toward the Divine life. The ego is afraid it will lose something of its privileges if it were to acknowledge soul as its master. Ego does not want to extinguish itself, and I don't want to suggest that is what I am trying to promulgate.

The ego isn't "good" or bad," it simply IS. We just need to recognize that the ego is simply a tool for our survival in this world. It helps us to make choices, decisions, setting boundaries, striving to become better at our jobs, creating art, music, inventions, and many other skills that contribute to our worldly existence.

As long as we are in control of our egos, it will work for us. But as soon as our ego starts going out of our control, it will hurt us if we are being too caught up with its' drama on this material plane. Our ego believes we are "separate" from others and life itself. Some people are rich, others are poor; some people are skinny, others are obese; some are highly intellectual, others have very low IQ's. Some people live "good" lives and others "bad" lives. Do you see the duality that our egos teach us about how separate we are from one another? As a result, our egos judge those who are different from us, often times alienating ourselves from others.

We are so used to worry, fear, anxiety, remorse, guilt, and conflict as normal life. Those feelings are all ego-based and one can fall into the temptation of feeling sorry for oneself, or angry, or worried. Few people suspect that there is actually any other option.

There is an option that is always available, but to be experienced, it must be chosen above all other options. This is what the mystical path is all about. Choosing to live from a state of ignorance and ego's fear-based attachments or choosing to live from the experience of the presence of God always available and present within at all times, but awaits choice. That choice is made only by surrendering everything other than peace and love to God.

I wish I can make everyone's doubts about what I am saying subside so what I talk about can be realized. Heaven is truly within and is revealed by *awareness*. Hidden within are the secrets of our Beloved's message for us to use to enhance our lives. We read about them; we hear them uttered, but we cannot possibly comprehend their meaning unless we have direct experience of their truth. How can we discover what our soul desires we learn? We can use meditation, prayer, dreams, synchronicity, quiet time, observing and listening to what nature is showing us, and being observant to our soul's subconscious messages.

The mystics and saints of the past help us in this quest. What they all have in common is their surrender to something beyond themselves so their intense spiritual discipline allowed them to achieve some perfection in their ability to love and care for others. Through their writings, we are reminded that we all have the potential to pursue and attain a similar character.

"Employ your time in improving yourself by other men's writings, so that you shall gain easily what others have labored hard for."

–Socrates

CHAPTER 6
NDES AS SEED EXPERIENCES

While mystical near-death experiences have a great deal to teach us about life after death, I take an additional viewpoint. Near-death experiences and other spiritually transformative experiences are initial seed experiences, the first stage of a long term process of developing one's consciousness toward unitive consciousness or oneness with God. It is the first step as an individual's direct encounter with an aspect of reality which is normally concealed from every day experience of the sense world.

Those of us who have had near-death experiences remember the day we received that most precious gift. We tapped into the ultimate truth that the saints and sages of the past searched for. For a few moments, we moved out of our chaotic world into the peaceful environment of a transcendent reality. For many of us, the door to that reality unlocked feelings we experienced as indescribable. What we experienced cannot be communicated in words, although we try.

There is a Chinese saying:

"Only the person who drinks the water can tell how warm or cool it is."

Having a near-death experience is just the beginning of cultivating and realizing the vast potential we now have within us. We still need to make an effort to learn and grow toward an even higher state of consciousness that we were initially awakened to during our near-death experience.

All spiritual experiences have value if they lead the experiencer to move toward union with the Divine forever, and act as a liason between the things on earth and the things in eternity. However, many near-death experiencers although having had a mystical experience, have not attained the heights of spiritual consciousness that the perfected mystics and saints have reached. Having a mystical experience is not the same as *being* a mystic. The difference between the mystic and someone else is this: The true mystic seeks to live his life in a complete and intimate relationship with God. He stands on earth, but his head is in heaven.

Evelyn Underhill wrote,

"The mystic dwells in a world unknown to other men. He pierces the veil of imperfection, and beholds Creation with the Creator's eye."

Flashes of insights into the glorious visions and knowledge that many near-death experiencers have had, are but a taste of the spiritual world being revealed to them. They may still have blinders on to seeing the ultimate nature of existence and union with God. As long as we are focused on what a neat experience we had, we enter into a trap of what is called "spiritual materialism," a term coined by Chogyam Trungpa. Our egos can feed off that near-death experience generating feelings of superiority or developing a "holier-than-thou" attitude. Even though we have had mystical near-death experiences – lights, visions, they are not genuine self-transcendence or God-realization. They are merely the awakening experiences preparing us for further stages of spiritual development toward the ultimate unitive experience.

The ego loves to be praised and to be in the spotlight, and near-death experiences give us that opportunity. By clinging to this self-identity, we risk not moving forward from the near-death experience along the path toward the unitive experience. If we don't heed the call to *progress* in our spiritual awakening that occurred during the near-death experience, we will never be able to find the most perfect union with God.

The essence of Truth and kinship with the Beloved will become clearer as we work toward uncovering the obscurities of our physical desires related to our senses. We desire what the eye sees, what the ears hear, what the nose smells and what the mouth can eat and speak. All these desires confuse our spiritual heart. If we pay more attention to the ego path of the senses, our spirit will be like a ship that has gone down at sea. But if we can continue on the path that awakened us to a higher consciousness and allow the Divine presence within to govern our lives, it is then possible to live as a liberated soul.

Thankfully, we have the mystics and saints who came before us and whose jewels of mystical literature glow with the intimate and impassioned love of God. Their teachings convey the message of awakening the God (the soul) within each of us. The love they speak of is a love that makes one's heart transparent and pure to the extent that the heart is revealed in the outer and inner worlds. It is then that the heart of love is able to communicate with others and with God. This is not a task that we will ever completely finish or master. It is a practice, an art, a signpost of what to be aware of as we evolve and open our hearts day by day.

Each one of us has been bestowed a soul given to us by the Creator. If we act in accordance with our true nature, then we are acting in accordance with the Divine Plan for our lives. No matter who we are, or where we come from, each soul is unique in its creation. Each soul is precious.

> *"I saw that every flower He has created has a beauty of its own, that the splendor of the rose and the lily's whiteness do not deprive the violet of its scent nor make less ravishing the daisy's charm. I saw that if every flower wished to be a rose, Nature would lose her spring adornments, and the fields would be no longer enameled with their varied flowers."*
>
> –St. Therese of Lisieux

It is really up to us to continue walking the path toward manifesting our truest virtues, each one of us, a flower of God's creation. The mystical path is the heavenly truth, the most precious spiritual teaching that has been available to human beings since ancient times.

The path is long and hard. But if we genuinely desire to turn to God within to nourish our seed of potentiality, we will see the seed reaping the fruit of spiritual growth from one stage to the next. Then perhaps one day, the unitive experience will present itself as God's gift of grace to us where we will be able to realize **direct contact or union with God.** We cannot hasten our spiritual growth by willfully trying to induce the unitive experience. It won't work. The unitive experience comes to us only by God's grace.

What we can do however, is pray by silently turning toward God acknowledging our desires to have our will be as God's Will. We can practice living the spiritual reality as best we can with humility and gratitude. It means trusting the Source whether or not we feel it rather than retreating into our conditioned life style. Seeing God in all things, regardless of whether the thing is great or small, ordinary or extraordinary, and then expressing that insight through selfless service. Above all, seeking every opportunity to love God, self and others unconditionally as best we can.

We may never receive that rare unitive experience in this lifetime, but perhaps by working actively progressing from the lower to the higher stages of consciousness, we may be preparing ourselves to receive it during another lifetime. In the process, the seed we sow now, will produce a meaningful and fulfilling life. Remember, that the value of life is not determined by its length, but by the quality of its inner essence and substance.

"Whoever sows sparingly will also reap sparingly, and whoever sows generously will also reap generously."
—Apostle Paul

CHAPTER 7
PREPARING FOR
THE MYSTICAL PATH

In the book, The Cloud of Unknowing, written by an anonymous English monk during the fourteenth century, it describes the beginning of the mystical journey as a longing to awakening, as in the words,

"In fact, anyone who longs for heaven is already there in spirit. The highway to heaven is measured by desires, not by feet. Our longing is the most direct route."

In preparing for the mystical path, it is important to understand that the instructions are not meant to make one holy by something we do. Rather, it is a *state* we enter. The path is a path toward love, healing and living an abundant life.

There are no coincidences in life. All events that take place have ultimate growth powers for the unfolding of our potential as human beings. While on the other side with my Beloved, I learned that our lives have been predetermined while we were in spirit form before birth. We came to earth school to learn the lessons we wanted to learn in order that we would progress in experiencing a deeper interior life by living from our true self.

We all have egos that shout, *"This isn't fair; someone abused me; I have a right to be furious at some people for the way they treated me."* I could go on citing many instances that infuriate us. We feel justified in wanting to avenge our anger. It's so easy to claim that we didn't sign up for all this unsettling stuff. Because we have no memory of our agreed upon plan before we were born into this world, It is our ego that creates the needless conflict.

When I was on the other side with my Great Teacher, I learned that souls who share the same vibration share the same realm on the other side. In order to ascend and remain in union with God when we die, our spiritual vibration must be very high. Earth school is the realm where opportunities overflow for the individual to create the spiritual progress that will increase our spiritual vibration. That is why it is so imperative that we don't just sit back and not make use of those opportunities to grow in the fullness of our spiritual potential. Life presents us with many difficulties and hardships. The wise person should ask themselves what it is that can be learned from one's journey through life that will return the soul to the inner activities of the Spirit.

We are always on the mystical path toward oneness with God. Gradually, we come to realize that we are that place in consciousness where God shines through us. We feel an inner warmth, a living presence, a Divine assurance. This reality becomes a habitual state of consciousness, a constant awareness of Truth, relying on Divinity unfolding and revealing Itself as us. Learning to be receptive to this Divinity within us, and expressing that Divinity outwardly from us, we develop the attributes of a God-consciousness necessary for ultimate union with God.

When we die and leave the physical body, the soul will be attracted to the specific realm that correlates with its specific level of consciousness. If we have not developed our spiritual vibration enough to enter the higher realms, we will always be given additional opportunities to develop that higher consciousness either reincarnating to the earth plane to do it all over again, or being given opportunities in the spiritual realms. My understanding is that we learn faster in earth school, hence the reason we choose to learn our lessons here.

The path toward ultimate union with God can be arduous and demanding. But it can become easier when we let the love for God replace the willfulness that is driving us.

I was one of those individuals who felt I was justified in becoming angry or frustrated over someone's actions if they offended me. The turning point was when I had my unitive experience with my Beloved. Because I had entered a state of non-ego, and only Divine Love was experiencing itself through me, I understood the meaning and purpose of life. I accepted as truth, all that my Beloved taught me. I was convinced then and now, that we are all on a Divine journey that is powerful, uncompromising, and yet so simple. Nothing is left to chance.

I know – I mean *I really know* that everyone is being watched over through every passageway we are invited to traverse. It is our choice to determine if we want to live in a quiet inner space or one fraught with pain and sorrow dominated by the ego's loud voice. The bossy ego can easily block our awareness of love because the ego is fearful and can never know love. It wants to matter above all, taking charge of our thoughts and our actions in ways that reflect fear. All too often, we listen to it rather than to acknowledge the very quiet, very kind, very loving voice which will always speak truth, unlike the ego's negative and sometimes destructive voice.

Before my unitive experience, I knew absolutely nothing at all about the ego and its control over our lives. My Beloved taught me during my unitive experience about the loud clamoring voice of the ego and the still small voice of the Holy Spirit. Everything I was being taught was as clear and refreshing to my consciousness as cool well-water to thirsty lips. This knowledge was given to me as a gift to share with humanity. I learned a great deal of spiritual knowledge not from books, teachers, workshops, or from any other source other than from my Beloved on that gifted day of January 29, 1979.

That was the reason I never wanted to purposely read books about spiritual matters once I returned from my unitive experience. I wanted to stay true to only what my Beloved taught me during my unitive experience. In that way, it proved to me that the knowledge I received was truthful to its core and coming from no other source except my Beloved. In order for truth to be known, it must be *directly experienced!*

Through the years, some people have asked me if I ever read *A Course in Miracles* because they said that what I describe is what the *Course in Miracles* teaches. My answer is no, I never read *A Course in Miracles* and I never plan on reading it. Let me explain.

In the early 1980's, I had the opportunity to attend a national board meeting for the International Association for Near-Death Studies held in Washington, D.C. All the board members were housed and entertained at the president of the organization's very nice home. The library was an enormous room lined with bookcases on all the walls.

Here and there a solitary book greeted me like a friend in a crowd of strange faces. One thin book stuck out from the rest of the neatly arranged books on one shelf, just sticking out enough to catch my attention. The book was titled, *"A Teacher's Manual for A Course in Miracles."*

I flipped the book open to see what it was and after reading just a few sentences, I became very excited. A board member approached me and told me he noticed how excited I seemed to be reading the book and he said to me, *"I see you are reading A Course in Miracles. Have you ever read the Course before?"* I didn't know what he was referring to. I never heard of *"A Course in Miracles."* Was it some college "course" or some other type of course like that? I didn't know.

"No, I replied. I never read this book before, but the few sentences I read, is exactly what I learned during my near-death-like experience," I told him. He then told me how *A Course in Miracles* was written, actually through automatic writing through the vessel of psychologist, Helen Schucman during the 1970's. Apparently, it has become a classic book on transformation.

I immediately decided at that moment that I would never read the book or any other books that teach what my Great Teacher revealed to me through direct revelation. If what I teach does not come from books or from any other medium except through my own revelations, then where does my knowledge come from? It's just my own way of staying true to what my Great Teacher personally revealed to me, that's all. But when I come upon the same revelations being brought forth by others, it is a wonderful feeling knowing that information came to me from no other source other than my Beloved. Silently, I give thanks to my Great Teacher.

Then the day came when the title of this book passed through my mind the winter of 2018 bringing up the word "unitive experience," a term I never heard before. I understood that if God was calling me to write this book, I had to become familiar with the mystics and saints who purportedly, as my friend told me, had similar experiences that I had with God. Thus began my search through the extensive literature on the subject so I would be able to garner the information about the mystics and saints who shared the unitive experience with me.

Most of the spiritual writing that I am doing for this book comes from the memory of the knowledge that my Beloved "downloaded" into my consciousness during my union with God. Total knowledge was revealed to me and seems to appear when I am writing in order to help others in some way. However, I cannot recall all knowledge on cue. The gift I have seems to appear **only when I write with my co-author, God.** When I finish writing my books, I cannot remember what I wrote. When I re-read my books, it is as if I am reading a book written by someone else because during my ordinary consciousness, I do not speak or write this way. I know myself better than anyone else, and when I say that normally, I cannot write like this, I mean it!

Before I write my books, I always pray first and enter into a very deep communion with my Great Teacher, God. I allow my will to be God's Will, thus being consumed with His Love as my writing unfolds. My consciousness becomes elevated beyond my normal consciousness as I enter into this partnership with God that will bring forth the words and message that I have been given. With faith in my inner guidance, I seek only to write in such a way that I glorify God. Such is the great joy of the Eternal One.

Even though I was given total knowledge during my

experience, I can't recall for instance, the cure for cancer and other knowledge I was given at that time. I'm not supposed to remember everything I guess. The knowledge surfaces only when it seems I am permitted to recall it for some higher purpose.

For most people, there is an external search for happiness. We have moments of happiness, but they aren't lasting. As fleeting as a bird on wing, those moments disappear quickly and out of sight. It's unsettling thinking that everyone else has a good life except us. Fortunately, no matter how many times we have tried and failed, or how many times what others have done to us or said about us, we still have the longing that lies inside us to guide us to the realm of possibility.

The Divine Presence within holds our capacity for knowing, loving, and choosing a different path, one which, if followed, will lead us to inner peace which is at the heart of everything. Seeking the peace of the Holy Spirit whose job it is to guide us freedom from anxiety and conflict is the choice we must make to un-complicate our lives. It is the path toward union with God.

It has become so much easier for me to listen to the softer loving guidance of the voice of the Holy Spirit within to release the insanity of the ego when it wants to exhibit control over me. At one time my ego would have encouraged me to lash out against others who lashed out against me. But now, thinking back of several individuals whose malicious behavior towards me prompted me to react with kindness in trying to resolve the issues with those individuals was the healthy and loving way to deal with those problems. I came with an open heart giving energetically and emotionally to them, feeling joy that I was helping them to move forward with their goals. It was about helping *them, no strings attached.* Their egos refused however, to allow them to see the situations from a different perspective. The result was that they went on their way with rage in their hearts while I went on my way with peace in my heart knowing I acted out of love. The baffling part of all this was that those individuals were near-death experiencers.

At first my ego judged them for thinking that all near-death experiencers automatically returned from their experiences as I did, loving one another and doing no harm to anyone. Their behaviors confused me until I realized they were listening to the strong-armed, loud ego's voice which they chose to act from. Ego is always jockeying to feel above, or better than others. Those who walk the pathway of fear consider themselves "tough and strong," and their egos are threatened by anything soft, so they push away the love that is offered them. Hanging on to the anger or hate is a harsh way of living. One can find no true peace when unloving intentions have made their home in one's heart.

The outer world reflects our inner world; please remember that. Fear based actions are a lower vibrational energy which will always be met with less satisfaction in life. Love based actions are a higher vibrational energy which will always be met with great satisfaction in life. The act of giving from love is always Divinely guided and is so joyful that it is its own reward.

Coming from a place of love is our purpose fulfilled. During my unitive experience, my true self merged and was one with God. Only love is real, the rest is an illusion. We forgot who we are —one with God, a being of pure Divine Love. Everyone without exception is a beloved child of God, resting within God's mind and heart. In our forgetfulness, we have allowed our ego to act from a place of victimhood, powerlessness, and suffering. For this reason, it is easy to feel that God is far away and too busy to get involved with us.

However, when we follow the voice of the Holy Spirit within which always leads us along the pathway of love, we receive the support from God in the form of beautiful experiences and our needs being met. When we react to life's situations with love, we feel that familiar Heavenly warmth as if being wrapped by a warm and fuzzy blanket. When we react to life's situations from fear, we feel abandoned by God, and others. Our fears allow us to make fear-based decisions which are self-inflicted modes of pain and suffering.

"Fear is such a powerful emotion for humans that when we allow it to take us over, it drives compassion right out of our hearts."

–St. Francis Aquinas

So what can we do to tame the ego's fear energy that seems to have taken hold over us? Love is the answer. Become aware that one's real self is God-given endowed with a Heavenly consciousness that can overcome any of ego's adversity.

"Man says...Show me and I'll trust you. God says... Trust me and I'll show you."

–Psalm 126-6

Divine Love is the restorative healer for anyone wishing to overcome ego's agenda of fear. Divine Love is already available to us in the depths of our souls. We simply need to acknowledge that it exists there and that we have access to that loving healer.

The peace prayer of Saint Francis of Assisi asks that we

may be instruments of peace in the midst of hatred, doubt, injury, despair, sadness, and darkness. The prayer doesn't ask that those difficult circumstances be taken away. It only asks that we radiate peace when confronted with them. The action of love in any situation will always bring peace.

If the ego is struggling to overpower our thoughts with fear, send it love. Ask Divine Presence within for assistance in bringing up the soul's power of love so that healing can occur. Trying to fix fear thoughts from one's lower self won't work. The only way to fix anything is from one's higher self, whose connection to God and solutions is immediate.

Life teaches us that often, we cannot free ourselves on our own. Sometimes I have been successful, but sometimes I fail or I have to ask for help. We are willful humans aren't we? We want to appear strong enough to be able to control our outer circumstances, and hold onto our attachments of pride, judgement, deceit, or a host of other ego-centered traits, believing that spiritual matters can be achieved by the intellect and will power. However, until we have exhausted our own efforts and become open to God's longing for us and our longing for God, we will never realize the sweet call to love, the call to let go of all in us that is not love so that we can fully participate in the ever-present communion of the Divine reality.

"You have to keep breaking your heart until it OPENS."
                                                        –Rumi

Saint John of the Cross tells us that God's grace flows through us the more we empty ourselves of the attachments to anything that restricts our openness to that divine reality. All great spirituality is about letting go.

If we try to work out spirituality in our heads, it won't work. However, when we begin to *"love with our whole heart, our whole soul, our whole mind, and our whole strength,"* (Mark 12:30), that's when we have a much stronger possibility of surrendering our ego controls and engaging into the transformation available to every human being that God created.

When I read the poem of Saint John of the Cross, it brought tears to my eyes as I recalled during my unitive experience that moment when by grace, I learned the truth about myself as seen through God's eyes. I'd like to share that poem with you in the hope that as you read those beautiful words, it will invite you to sit in silence for a few moments remembering who you are- someone created in the image and likeness of the Divine Presence within you. Soak in that luminous, resonant truth about yourself and our Beloved.

When you regarded me
Your eyes imprinted your grace in me,
In this, you loved me again,
And thus my eyes merited
To also love what you see in me...
Let us go forth together to see ourselves in Your beauty.

CHAPTER 8

THE INVISIBLE LIFE

Who we are is invisible to the eyes. Yes, we have fleshy bodies, but that unknown feature we call Spirit, that unknown Presence we call God the Creator, is at work among the particles of matter; forming, revealing, intensifying, spiritualizing, evolving. Truly, we should rejoice that God has given us the opportunity to partake of the right to become One with Him, and to reveal one by one, His glorious ideals.

Our real and gifted selves are flashing with Spirit awaiting our hearts and minds to the awareness of who we are. The consciousness of the One who resides within the depth of our being, awaits our choice to accept the Holy guidance which our Beloved wishes to express in and through us.

As we become more aware of our Divine Self, Divine Love flows through us to bring us to the perfection of ourselves, making us whole. I want nothing more than to guide others into their awareness of their true selves so they will know that our Beloved dwells within the center of our being. The indwelling God loves every cell of our being. When we know that every part of our being is impregnated with Holy Light, we will not judge ourselves or condemn any part of our being.

When we know that our Beloved Self is breathing through us, thinking through us, loving through us, radiating from us, we won't doubt our own power. Oh, the joy of knowing how beautiful this Holy Self feels within us. How beautiful it is to observe how we are able to move forward in grace. How beautiful it is to watch how we begin to communicate on a higher level, as we tune into our Divine Nature and call forth the Divinity in all those around us. For as we know our true nature, we know the true nature of every man, woman and child in the universe.

Love your true nature with all your heart; it is a cherished gift. Give of it wherever you go, so that all may be lifted into a greater awareness of their Divine Nature. To deny love is to deny God.

Deep within, deep within the surface of the mind, beyond the intellect, in a mysterious place within each and every one of us is found the meaning and purpose of our lives. We were given this knowledge before we were born into this world and it will be with us when we leave this world. God has given humanity great teachings to help us to evolve into the greater purpose for which we were created. It is up to us to find and follow what God has sent us here to do, and that is something our intellect cannot discern. It is something intrinsic within us that is waiting to be discovered.

In order to discover this mysterious place, to discover God, and to discover our purpose, we have to start developing qualities slowly within ourselves. These qualities are compassion, forgiveness, and tolerance. Love would be the key that opens the door to discovering the Divine within and all that is waiting to be revealed.

To reach God within, all that is needed is faith and surrender. This longing and deep stirrings that may begin to form in our heart is evidence of what Saint Augustine said in his prayer at the beginning of his autobiographical *Confessions*:

"You (O God) have made us for yourself, and our heart is restless until it rests in you."

We were created for the mystical path toward wholeness and oneness with God, the most important journey we will ever take. Along the way, we will meet others who will play an important role who perhaps unknowingly, will lead us forward to navigate the uncertain times ahead. Some people may mentor us; some have traveled the path we are on and can support us. Every step we take, every opportunity that arises, every person who crosses our path allows us to achieve selfless intention and action which the higher spiritual life demands. Celebrate all those catalysts that are meant to help you move along the mystical path toward God. Those catalysts that have been orchestrated by God are summoning us from one level to another.

J. Krishnamurti said:

"There are many people who will tell you the purpose of life; they will tell you what the sacred books say. Clever people will go on inventing various purposes of life. The political group will have one purpose, the religious group will have another, and so on and on. And how are you to find out what is the purpose of life when you yourself are confused? Surely, as long as you are confused, you can only receive an answer which is also confused. If your mind is disturbed, if it is not really quiet, whatever answer you receive will be through this screen of confusion,

anxiety, fear; therefore the answer will be perverted. So the important thing is not to ask what is the purpose of life, but to clear away the confusion that is within you. It is like a blind man asking, "What is light?" If I try to tell him what light is, he will listen according to his blindness, according to his darkness; but from the moment he is able to see, he will never ask what is light. It is there."

Only God knows what is coming over the horizon. God's vantage point includes so much more than human eyes are capable of seeing. We must prepare ourselves to be receptive and sensitive to the Divine Presence within whose soft voice is slowly awakening our spiritual senses. Most of the time we don't even know what is happening inside of us. We are generally clueless to what our Beloved is working on and weaving behind the scenes. We will get frustrated at times and think of throwing in the towel on this mystical path we are on. Yet there is something pushing us. Something is compelling us to keep going.

"When you accept God's Will in every aspect of your life you will find God providing you with strength, courage, and a dignity that resounds to the heavens. It resounds to the heavens because it doesn't have far to go. Heaven, you see, is suddenly in your heart."

–Mother Angelica

If we pay attention, clear our mind and be open to discernment, we open the channel from the core of our inner Being where we can receive the guidance necessary to actualize our potential for living a sacred life. As our understanding increases, ignorance dissipates and we can modify our motives, outgrowing the selfish ones.

The soul knows God and all spiritual things. But the soul must awaken first, otherwise it really doesn't know God. You can be religious, but you don't encounter God at any depth. Many religions don't teach people how to have an *experiential* connection with our Beloved, so many end up not having a deep relationship with God. That is why it is so important to stay on the mystical path so we can connect with our indescribable, beautiful True Self.

I promise you that once you see things from a higher dimension, you see what you had not seen before. When that gift is released what's inside you, there is no going back. You can try, but your plan won't work because you cannot fathom going back to the old ways. That may have satisfied you before, but once God's Love and Power revealed itself to you, you only want to look forward to the next glory.

Rainer Maria Rilke wrote:

"A billion stars go spinning through the night, glittering above your head
But in you is the presence that will be
When all the stars are dead."

CHAPTER 9
AWAKENING

It is difficult for us to see ourselves as we really are. We have been conditioned most of our lives to view our physical reality as the "real reality." We think we know ourselves very well. From one point of view we may. Within us we have a record or memory of all we have done and all that has happened to us since we were born. Encoded in our brain is the wisdom and dreams of tomorrow and the desire for communion and community. Language and all great achievements emerge from the complex interaction of billions of neurons. If we think we understand ourselves based on all that information we have gleaned over our lifetime, then you don't need this book.

But I believe that everyone can reach their potential when the personality comes into its own wholeness of being. By learning that we have a dual nature, a material body occupied and energized by a spiritual essence we can transform an ordinary life into a miraculous life.

This isn't a new idea by any means. It is basic to all major religions, most of which call the internal essence the "soul." There is a place within us that longs for something more than the lives we have created for ourselves. I'm not talking about more possessions, honors, or even money. The longing I'm talking about is beyond labels and possessions. The usual definition of this internal essence or the soul is that it is the fundamental principle of life. That's what Aristotle called it, five centuries before Christ.

Before my unitive experience, I did not know that God's Presence was found within one's human self. I had always believed that God lived in Heaven, or as I was taught as a child, God lives in the Catholic Church in the tabernacle. I was very surprised to learn from my Great Teacher that we all have the very presence of our Beloved **within us.**

So much of my writing focuses on that simple truth because this is such a huge revelation and I want to shout it to the rooftops. Even though God is big enough to rule the entire universe, He is small enough to live in our hearts. To know that we are the fulfillment of God, that we are that place in consciousness where our Beloved shines through, is a remarkable gift we have been given. *"The kingdom of God is within you."* Luke 17:21

It was Saint Augustine who once said that he had lost much time in the beginning of his Christian experience by trying to find the Lord outwardly rather than by turning inwardly. I too, learned that God's Truth is not a religious system, but a way of life. The mystical path toward union with God which I am writing about is all about developing ourselves toward a higher faculty of consciousness whereby we love ourselves and *all* others from an inner awareness and trust of love. This comes about through a power born of an intimate relationship with God.

Not only is the soul considered the principle of life; it is also the source of our unique human life. A soul has the ability to experience and to imagine much more than our senses can offer. Having transcended our five senses, our soul brings to us reality in place of the finite sense of existence. However, our awareness of our soul's voice within is in direct proportion to how receptive and responsive we are to its quiet and soft voice.

Soul will always guide us to live out from the center of our being. It is the *giving* sense rather than *getting; being* rather than *attaining*.

As Evelyn Underhill points out:

"Mysticism, in its pure form, is the science of ultimates, the science of union with the Absolute, and nothing else, and that the mystic is the person who attains to this union, not the person who talks about it. Not to know about, but to Be, is the mark of the real initiate."

Some of us became aware of our mystical nature suddenly, unbidden and unsought, as in the case with near-death experiences. Even though the experience was spontaneous and revealed a reality of an altered perception, some individuals go no further along the path toward union with God, instead, basking in the memory of their beautiful mystical experience.

One woman in my study of *Ordinary People Having Spiritually Transformative Experiences* told me, *"I haven't been able to get to that same place again in my meditation where I saw the Light. I try so hard."* The problem is that she was trying to rekindle the feeling through an effort of her self-will. True, some people do have meaningful experiences while meditating, and they may be called mystical, but they may not reach full realization of the awareness that defines authentic mysticism. Authentic mystical experience suggests complete transcendence of the separate self-sense and awakening awareness of non-duality, a sense of pure Being.

Mystical experiences occur spontaneously, not by willful force. The will is ego, and when ego gets involved, it always prevents or ruins beautiful experiences. One of the drawbacks to seeking the mystical experience through training the will through discipline and concentration in an effort to gain power and knowledge is that such training feeds intellectual arrogance and neglects love.

True mystical experience, no matter how it presents to the individual, is an ecstatic dissolution of all ego boundaries. This has a healing effect upon the psyche. The mystic is one who desires to know, that they may love, and their desire for union is founded neither on curiosity nor self-interest. That is why lasting bliss comes with developing the mystical traits that live beyond the ego.

How does true mystical experience differ from psychic experience? Even though a psychic experience transcends ordinary confines of time and space, it does not usually transcend the separate self-sense. A psychic observer reports and interprets what is observed and is often goal directed. A psychic reader for instance, is working in the realm of duality and perception. In true mystical experience, both duality and perception are transcended. With mystical experience there is the feeling of being awakened to bliss-consciousness, an ecstatic dissolution of all ego boundaries.

Awakening to a state of mystical consciousness that many near-death experiencers awakened to, is not the same as living continuously in a state of mystical consciousness. Becoming a mystic is a lifelong task of cultivating awareness and learning to perceive love and an interconnectedness in all things. Even though many people have had mystical experiences, it is easy to fall back into the trappings of ego as we become witnesses in the world of human events. Throughout one's lifetime, the ego-self has been the focus of one's endeavors; therefore, the emotional investment in it has been enormous. The ego is both the source and the object of striving and is heavily imbued with sentiment as well as the whole gamut of human feelings, failings, gains and losses, victories and tragedies.

With so much invested in this ego-entity, it seems too valuable to relinquish. The ego clings to all its faculties because it wants to survive at all costs. It has endless schemes for enhancing survival which is based on the fear of loss. One of the biggest reasons why people do not stay on the path toward mystical union with God is that they are only "curious" about it and not "serious" about it. Also, people do not accept what is said; they're only interested in arguing against what is stated. Again, that's the ego rising in the mind of the individual wanting to be in charge.

To live the life of a mystic does not mean we have to kill the ego. The only thing we need to do is to let go of the identification with the ego as one's real self! To let go of the ego's control over us is no simple task. It appears to take great courage and resolve to transcend the goal seeking of the ego.

I believe we cannot transcend the ego without God's help. This means a willingness to "sacrifice" all the traits of the ego to God out of love and humility. A good approach is to let the love for God replace the willfulness that is driving the seeking. To be a perfect channel for God's Love is to welcome the joy which itself becomes the initiator of further spiritual work.

I know this to be very true because on my own, with my ego trying to write this book, I cannot write. I learned many years ago when I first began to write that in order to be a channel for God's Love to others through the books I write, I had to put my ego on a shelf, out of my way. Then through prayer and communion with God, only then does my writing takes form. From joy and humility, the rest of the spiritual work I do is certain.

God works best when we come to the end of ourselves with the willingness to ask for His Help.

"Why do you stay in prison when the door is so wide open?"

−Rumi

CHAPTER 10
DIVINE ENERGY

Humans all have a dual nature, a material physical body occupied and one energized by a spiritual essence, called the "soul." We use physical energy to maintain our physical body with nourishment in the form of what we eat and drink, and from the air that we breathe. Everything that we can see, feel, smell, hear or taste is a form of vibrating energy, confirmed by the scientific community. All physical matter is made up of atoms which in turn are composed of electrons and protons and neutrons all moving as vibrating energy.

Science believes, with very good reason, that everything in the physical universe is energy. Officially, at least, science does not recognize anything which is not measurable. What we may refer to as heaven, for instance, has no place in conventional science, and therefore could not yet be defined as energy. I go beyond that thought because I personally experienced the invisible world including God as energy. I understood that the power of God flows through us and the entire universe as being expressed as a very high form of energy. It is of a higher frequency than our instruments have identified.

I should add however, that there are some very great investigators and theoretical physicists who are moving beyond our Newtonian concepts of space and time that makes us look at reality in a completely different way.

There is now a willingness to investigate and take seriously, the many accounts of individuals whose personal stories and subjective experiences are essential sources of evidence.

The physical world vibrates at a relatively slow rate but as you get away from it to higher levels, this vibratory rate increases, while the composition becomes finer. This finer energy is all around us, yet, invisible. In it "we live and have our being." Our body is what we are; our soul is who we are.

Energy cannot be seen, only results of its actions may be seen. This God Power that flows is undifferentiated, that is to say, of itself it is not flesh or bones or music or poetry or icebergs or minerals or air – rather, it is the very essence of life – life containing all potentiality, each center of individualized life – and that includes each person. Each center acts as a filter and transposes that power through its own individual intention and in accordance with the filter that it has become. Filters come in all sizes, shapes and patterns – like cookie cutters, for instance.

Some may object that this description of God as energy eliminates a personal God. My definition of a "personal God" is not one which maintains God is a person but one in which God is real, very real, to each one of us. Our appeals to God are heard but the answers must come through His creations. In this view God is revealed through His creations since every one of them is a part of Him.

One example of how God revealed Himself through another, (and there have been lots), happened one time when my husband and I were driving to dinner one early evening. Whenever I get in a car, I always silently pray and ask God to protect us from harm and bring us safely to our destination and back home again. It was a delightful summer's evening and we were driving in our small two passenger British Austin Healey sports car with the top down. My husband always drove the same deserted country road whenever we were going to drive into the city for any reason. I estimate our speed was 45-50 mph.

A crossroad was approaching, obscured by a few homes clustered together and among the tall evergreen trees that lined the road. We were just short of passing by the inter-section when my husband immediately turned the steering wheel hard, to the right and exclaimed, *"Let's go this way tonight instead of our usual way straight ahead."* He turned the steering wheel so sharply that my body was thrown into the passenger's door with such force that when my arm hit it I shouted, *"Ched, what are you doing?"*

What we both did not know at the time was that a speeding car had just arrived at the intersection at the **exact moment** my husband turned the steering wheel to drive down the other road, the road that speeding car came from. My husband was so shook up that he stopped the car until we both were able to recover from the shock of almost being in a crash that surely would have ended both our lives, or for certain my life. Had we driven straight ahead on the road we always travel, the other car would have slammed into the passenger seat where I was sitting. We both never saw that car coming! That driver drove right past the stop sign going at least 55 mph, if not faster.

What makes this story even more awesome is that my husband was an atheist. As we parked alongside the road waiting to recover from our near fatal car crash, I looked at my husband's ashen face and said, *"I have to pray right*

now Ched and thank God for saving our lives." I prayed with tears running down my cheeks, filled with gratitude that it wasn't our time to die. Ched's quivered voice exclaimed, *"What made me turn down this road at the last minute when I wasn't planning on driving down this road?"* I simply told him that God had answered my prayers to keep us safe. Shortly afterwards, we continued on our journey into the city for a relaxing dinner. Such is God's Grace and love that He would respond so quickly to save our lives. AND.......
He "spoke" to an atheist's soul to be the one who would hear his soul's inner voice to respond that quickly to avert a tragic accident. That's how God can "talk" to us without words. He doesn't mind using an atheist or a believer to show His immense Love for us! All are loved equally and without measure.

Here's another true story that reveals the manner in which our Beloved "speaks" to us.

One very cold spring morning, I was excited to go to a local garden center to buy some flowers for my garden. When I am at a garden center, I have a very hard time leaving because I am perusing every single flower trying to decide what to buy and where to plant new ones. I was gone from home perhaps four hours, losing track of time which is my norm at garden centers.

All of a sudden, like lightning fast speed, I had diarrhea. I had on cream colored slacks! There was no way I could run fast enough to a bathroom to hold it in. You guessed it......
disaster hit! I had to run out of the store, embarrassed to the hilt. When that accident happened, all I wanted to do was get home as fast as I could! When I got to my car, I covered the car seat with a plastic bag that was in the car so I could protect the seat when I sat on it.

When I pulled into the driveway, Ched called out to

me from behind the house. *"Nancy,* he shouted frantically, *"Come quickly! I need your help."*

I knew by the tone of his voice that it was more important for me to see what he needed than for me to go into the house and change my clothes. He was lying on the ground next to the fish pond. With a shocked expression on my face, he explained that he was leaning over to feed the fish, lost his balance, and fell into the pond head first. He had balance problems – peripheral neuropathy - as a complication of diabetes and a host of other issues. I always had to be close to him so he could lean on me when he started to walk or when he started to fall. My mind was racing with furious thoughts when I saw him lying on the ground. Why did he go outdoors to the fish pond by himself when I wasn't home? But I had no time to lecture him; I had to immediately tend to him.

He told me once he fell into the pond he couldn't get out and was struggling for forty-five minutes in the frigid water. Somehow while struggling to get out, he managed to crawl out onto the ground but couldn't go any further so he just laid there waiting for me to come home.

I tried to help him get on his feet but I couldn't get him to stand up. He was dead weight. Thinking quickly how to get him to stand up, I grabbed a chair from the patio and brought it to him. It took everything he had to support himself and stand up using the chair to brace himself. Once he was able to stand, I helped him to walk into the house where I cleaned him, put him to a nice warm bed, then I cleaned myself.

But as a wife, I wasted no time in scolding him for doing something while I wasn't home. We always had an agreement that if I was gone from the house, he had to sit and watch television or lie in bed until I came home. Ched had issues with seizures, so it was important that he remain in a safe place in the event a seizure would overtake him. But for some reason, he wanted to go to the fish pond probably thinking he would be okay by himself. Wrong!!

The worst part of all this is that Ched had a temporary catheter inserted near his neck where he received his dialysis treatments. He had to be extremely careful not to get it wet when he showered because of the bacteria in the water. We had well water. Those catheters had a very high infection rate and any bacteria that enters the catheter goes directly into the bloodstream and throughout the body. What do you think lying in a fish pond of skuzzy, bacteria infested water for forty-five minutes would do to him?

Ched was extremely lucky he didn't hit his head on the rocks that were at the bottom of the fish pond. He was also fortunate that the dialysis center was able to flush his line so nothing serious resulted.

When I was through scolding him, I told him that was the second time God was looking out for him and it was time he should be grateful to God. As an atheist, he didn't say anything. One wonders what was going on inside his head however. As for me, I can't help but think my diarrhea episode was brought about so that I would rush home to take care of Ched. Knowing how much I love to shop in a garden center, I'm sure I would have remained at least an hour longer. Imagine how Ched would have been lying on that cold dirt by the fish pond freezing in the forty degree weather and no one to help him. That was the first time I thanked God for giving me diarrhea!

Actually, there are thousands of cases which would show my point. I'm certain you have your own stories to share as well. The invisible field through which all energy flows instantaneously, explains how such occurrences happen. For a moment, fully accept the idea that we are one with God and that power is flowing through us at all times.

I have a point to make here and I will use a more limited living creature. I am going to say that the same power which flows through man also flows through the sparrow. I will begin the story with a sparrow which has just come to the point where it can fend for itself. When it becomes fully adult it will look for a mate and it will mate. Shortly the pair will build a nest, and when the eggs come, father and mother bird will take turns keeping them warm. When the little ones break through, the adults will begin gathering all kinds of tasty tidbits for their little ones. At a certain point in the babies' development they will be kicked out of the nest and they darn well better know how to fly. The parents will feed them a few more days and bid them goodbye, sometimes using force. And all of this will be accomplished by birds who never have done it before. What has happened is that the sparrow's filter has taken exactly what it needed from the flow of God and put it into practice. No "how-to" manuals at all. "Aha," you say, "but that was just instinct." My answer: "Aha, but where does instinct come from?" Instinct comes from the life beyond. It is not originated in RNA or DNA. It comes *through* them.

That same invisible power surged through my husband in a split second, warning him to steer the car in a different direction, thus, saving both our lives. That same invisible power surged through my colon in a split second, warning me that I needed to rush home immediately. I am suggesting that this is the same power that calls each of us to embark upon the mystical life. Unseen forces come to our aid. Grace appears.

"Once dust, you're now spirit,
Once ignorant, now wise.
He who had led you so far, will guide you further.

−Rumi

CHAPTER 11

BIOPHOTONS

During one part of my experience, the Light and I were taken back to the beginning of creation where I witnessed and understood that **everything** created sprang forth from the One Pure Light. All matter at its core from the smallest particles to the great cosmos are born of this Pure Light. I first began talking about this aspect of my experience shortly following my return to physical consciousness in 1979, even though at that time, I had no understanding of quantum physics. Nor did I learn from any other source other than directly from my own experience that the Light is to be found in all things.

We all have moments when in retrospect, a light bulb goes off in our brain and we become insightful into the nature of our human experiences, no matter how long ago those events happened. This happened to me several years following my career in cytology, (study of cells.)

For years I worked as a cytologist doing blood cancer research at a major university. I worked with a panel of twelve cytopathologists from the finest institutions around the country. Our purpose was to determine the validity of a theory proposed by Herbert Nieburgs, M.D. from Mt.

Sinai Hospital in New York, which if proven valid, could make a major contribution to the medical field.

I spent several weeks studying directly under Dr. Nieburgs to learn the morphology of the white blood cells which showed very specific light vacuoles lined up in the nucleus of the cell in a certain size and shape. These light configurations according to Dr. Nieburgs' theory would only show up in normal white blood cells as a precursor to the patient who would develop cancer at a later date. For all purposes, they were **normal cells**. They had not yet shown any atypical changes suggesting any abnormality in the cells. If Dr. Nieburgs' theory could be replicated by other investigators in other laboratories, then this theory called "malignancy associated changes" could become a valuable simple blood finger test to determine what patients could develop cancer in the future. Physicians would then monitor such patients more closely throughout their lives to detect the early signs of cancer.

The protocol we followed was strict as all scientific investigations must be. I set my laboratory up in such a way that that there would be no way in which I would know whose blood cells I was looking at under the microscope – a known cancer patient or a control, one without cancer. Someone other than myself drew the blood from a patient, stained the slides, and wrote a number on the end of the slide. It was then up to me to review the slides for the light vacuoles that Dr. Nieburgs taught me to see. I was getting 87% accurate diagnoses, being able to distinguish between the known cancer patients and the known controls. That was statistically significant.

Because of the success rate I was having, it was decided to set up a panel of other investigators who were cytopathologists from leading institutions around the country who were experts in analyzing cells. Dr. Nieburgs was in charge of the investigation. His laboratory collected the blood samples, stained the slides, labeled them with only a number on the end of each slide. Twelve slides per box were then sent to one of the twelve investigators to review and make a diagnosis whether the blood cells on the slides came from a cancer patient or a control patient. When finished, the box of slides were then sent to the next member of our investigative committee for diagnostic purposes.

I was the only one of the twelve cytopathologists who consistently reported the correct diagnosis. Why didn't the other cytopathologists see what I had observed? I presented my findings at a medical forum in New York with all the cytopathologists present. They grilled me to learn why I was able to see the light vacuoles and they couldn't. I didn't have an answer for them.

Because this experiment couldn't be replicated by other investigators, it was decided after several years that Dr. Nieburgs' theory wasn't something that was worth continuing on with that research. I have often thought of Dr. Nieburgs and how disappointed he must have been to see his theory go by the wayside because others could not replicate his theory.

Why were Dr. Nieburgs and I the only ones able to see those light vacuoles while twelve of the country's most elite cytopathologists couldn't observe them? I would like to speculate that the near-death experience that I had prior to working as a cytologist, activated my awareness so that I was able to recognize the light vacuoles in the nuclei of the blood cells. I don't know Dr. Nieburgs personal history, but perhaps there was something in his own "spiritual" background that he was able to see the light as I did. I will discuss this further in a moment.

Another instance of individuals perceiving light that others couldn't, happened when I was delivering the eulogy for my dear friend who died suddenly. It was during that eulogy service when I had my unitive experience with my Beloved. After the service, three women approached me separately who did not know each other. Each woman told me that as I was delivering the eulogy, a white light surrounded the outline of my entire body. The light was present during the entire fifteen minutes it took me to deliver the eulogy. One woman said when she saw the light, she thought it was something in her eyes so she rubbed them and when she opened them again, the light was still surrounding my entire body. I asked each woman privately if she was able to see auras, and each woman seemed to have a huge question mark on her face as if she didn't know what I was talking about. No, each woman knew nothing about auras, yet each saw a white glow surrounding my entire body as I spoke the entire duration of the eulogy. The eulogy if you recall, was when my unitive experience occurred. Hmm...

Recent scientific research has demonstrated that biophotons exist in the DNA of every living cell, and that they emit light. This may help to explain what I was able to see during my cancer research years and also to explain the light others saw around me while delivering the eulogy. So what are biophotons?

Biophotons are weak electromagnetic waves in the optical range of the spectrum – in other words, light. All living cells of plants, animals and human beings emit biophotons which cannot be seen by the naked eye. They can however, be measured by special equipment developed by German researchers. According to the biophoton theory, biophoton light is constantly being stored, released and absorbed by the DNA molecules of cellular nuclei. It is theorized that this biophoton light may connect cell organelles, cells, tissues, and organs within the body. They are generally believed to be produced as a result of energy metabolism within our cells.

In a couple of experiments scientists discovered that rat brains can pass just one biophoton per neuron a minute, but human brains could convert more than a billion biophotons per second.

Bear with me because what I am about to say may be even more exciting in terms of what this may mean for human consciousness and what many cultures refer to as Spirit. If there is light communication happening with biophotons our brains produce, then it raises the possibility that the more light one can produce and communicate between neurons, it can have strong implications that there is more to light than we are aware of.

Throughout history, saints and other sacred enlightened individuals were shown having glowing halos around their heads. Perhaps this light that circled their heads was a result of their higher consciousness and greater production of biophotons if there is any correlation between biophotons and consciousness, which I believe there is. Perhaps the more light we produce, the more we awaken and embody the wholeness of our Divine Consciousness.

Now I would like to introduce the reader to Mark Pitstick, D.C. He is director of The Soul Phone Foundation that supports the work of Dr. Gary Schwartz at the University of Arizona to enable spirit-communication with "departed" loved ones. Mark is also vice-president for Eternea, an organization merging science and spirituality started by Eben Alexander, M.D., and chaired by Professor Ervin Laszlo. Dr. Pitstick wrote the following testimony of an incident with me. In his own words:

"While filming the documentary Soul Proof in 2008, we interviewed many people who had firsthand experiences that suggest there is much more to life than can be perceived by human senses. This empirical evidence adds to the collective clinical and scientific evidence that consciousness/spirit is indeed eternal.

As Nancy shared her amazing NDE experience about waking up in the morgue, one of the camera crew noticed that her chest, neck, and face appeared blurred. A pendant hanging on her chest appears most out of focus. Furniture around her had normal definition as did her body below the chest. Attempts by the videographers to improve focus in those areas did not work and they had no explanation for why that might happen.

In some energy systems, the chest correlates with the 4th chakra, the throat with the 5th, and the glabella with the 6th. These are considered to be higher energy centers or vortexes that, respectively, are associated with higher love and compassion, awareness and communication, and abilities to heal and manifest.

Ten years later, my working hypothesis about this phenomenon has not changed: Nancy's energy is quite high and evolved in those areas. Those stronger energies may have interfered with normal photography in ways unknown to me.

After her NDE and NDE-like encounters, Nancy is more loving, empathetic, and vibrant than most humans. As anyone who knows her can sense, she radiates huge amounts of love and light. Perhaps that is what interfered with the camera images."

P.M.H. Atwater, a world noted NDE researcher who also had several NDEs, researched the aftereffects of near-death experiencers and found a common trait among us. We have problems with electronic equipment; lightbulbs burst in our presence, watches don't keep time, and a host of other sensitivities. She suggests that *"it is the intensity of the Light experienced, not the length of exposure that seems to determine the prevalence of many of the physiological aftereffects."*

She told me that her own energy is quite high and often times when she has appeared for interviews and workshops, she also experienced problems with microphones not working and overhead lights suddenly bursting. We chuckled when she said, *"that's God inside us wanting to be let out!"* I believe she is right. The Light is indeed God. When we get hyper-excited about God and feeling His Love within, our energy just explodes outwardly, bringing the Light with us.

As you can tell, I am spending some time on this subject of light and the mysteries that hide within the light. The light isn't a symbolic poetic reference. I argue that the Light is Divinity, the essence of Being. At least that was exactly how I perceived the Light during my near-death experience, and near-death-like unitive experience. Many other near-death experiencers have also believed this to be true based on what they also felt.

The human body is the most magnificent Light-Being there is! Raymond Moody, M.D., in his book, *The Light Beyond*, tells a story of one girl's father who had to free-dive forty feet in Puget Sound to save her. He is reported saying that the only way he was able to find her was because her physical body was glowing in white light.

William Bucke M.D., in his book *Cosmic Consciousness*, wrote about the stage of entering the final stage of enlightenment, the highest form of consciousness possessed by the ordinary man. He describes that it is *"the veritable transfiguration of the subject of the change as seen by others when the Cosmic sense is actually present."*

The dictionary describes *"transfiguration"* as a complete change of form or appearance into a more beautiful or spiritual state. The New Testament describes transfiguration as the sudden emanation of radiance from the person of Jesus.

Dante says that he was *"transhumanized into a God."* It appears that if he could have been seen at that moment he would have exhibited what could only have been called *"transfiguration."*

"When you possess light within, you see it externally."
—Anas Nin

What is the take-away point of all this? To realize that we are indeed Light within Light, the Divine in expression, the very Light of who we really are as souls. Perhaps biophotons which are found at all levels of higher and lower energy, allow us to bridge ourselves from slower realms of human consciousness to the faster and more synchronized realms of consciousness where we become more aware of our spiritual development toward wholeness.

CHAPTER 12
PROPHETIC DREAMS

Dreams can be a door that opens us to receive otherworldly messages. These surprises, which for the most part are unexpected gifts, can be plopped into our laps by a benevolent Presence.

Prophetic dreams are those dreams that I believe, moves the soul from the body of a person who is asleep and who visits real places and talks to real people, whether deceased or alive. This type of dream occurs only at a higher dimension where we are able to transcend time and space to observe the future. Sometimes knowledge or important information is revealed by a spiritual entity, God, angels, guides or some other highly evolved beings.

During sleep, that is the time when our conscious mind has been put to rest. It is the opportunity for our mind to be "awakened" not by waking up as when the morning sunshine bursts through the window calling us to get out of bed, but an awakening of a different nature.

"Indeed God speaks once, or twice, yet no one notices it – in a dream, a vision of the night. When sound asleep

falls on man, while they slumber in their beds. Then he opens the ears of men and seals their instruction."

–Job 33:14-16

I can usually tell the difference between a precognitive dream and an ordinary dream. A precognitive dream is felt with strong emotions and feels like it happened in "real time" making me feel I was at the exact spot or speaking to that exact person while I was asleep. Usually, I can't forget the precognitive dream easily like most ordinary dreams. The precognitive dream can stay with me for days, sometimes I never forget the dreams even years after they occurred. For me, many of my precognitive dreams predict something that will happen generally within a week or two of my dream. I will "see" the future event happening in my dream.

For instance, in 1986, while asleep, I had a dream of NASA's space shuttle lifting off from Cape Canaveral and exploding in the air after liftoff killing all seven crew members. In my dream, I saw the explosion exactly how it happened. The next day while watching the television of the space shuttle lifting off, I knew immediately, what was about to happen. I knew it would explode and it exploded exactly how I saw it in my dream.

Another time I had a dream that my mother had breast cancer. The next day my mother, who lived five hundred miles away, phoned me. *"Hello Nancy, how are you?"* she asked. Immediately, I said, *"Mother, don't tell me anything more. You have breast cancer in your left breast don't you?"* She was silent for a moment then asked me how I knew that because she just found out the bad news and was calling me to tell me. My dream had prepared me ahead of time for that news.

Another time I was dreaming about the airplane crash that killed John, our dear friend whose small plane crashed while he was flying over the Alaskan glaciers. During the dream, I saw that he was having difficulty with the controls and was not able to get control of the plane from spinning downward. At the last moment, he called out my name and the plane crashed. Early the next morning, his family member called me to tell me his plane crashed and he was dead.

These are just a few examples of many precognitive type dreams I have that foretell a future event.

I have also had many after-death communication dreams from deceased souls wanting to bring a message for me or for someone else.

Our dear friend John had a son who committed suicide. Unaware of Austin's death on the night of his suicide, I had a dream about him. In the dream, I was walking into his bedroom where he was sitting. The moment he saw me his eyes lit up and he bolted from his chair, embracing me with a big bear hug.

"Nancy," he said, "thank you so much for being such a good friend to me for all these years. I love you very much. You always loved me so unconditionally, and I want you to know how much I treasured that kind of love."

After we both exchanged words of loving friendship, he said, "I have to go now and go back to where I live."

I was confused because the scene was taking place in his bedroom. Seeing my confusion, he pointed to the sky above and said, "No, this is not where I live any longer." He pointed upward and when I looked up, the roof of his house was missing. I could see the vast universe with the stars and planets shining so brightly above. "That's where I live now," he said.

With a deep intuitive understanding, I knew what he was telling me. Then he flew upward into the dark universe while I watched him fade away. I understood that Austin felt it was very important to tell me how much he loved me and how important an influence I had been in his young life. The dream ended. When I woke up in the morning, I had that familiar feeling that this dream was no ordinary dream, but a message dream. A few hours later, his family member called to tell me he committed suicide *in his bedroom* during the night. This after death communication dream was a powerful testimony that time and space are no deterrents to eternal love and communication with our loved ones.

Quite intriguing are rare dreams called "shared dreams" where we share an identical dream with someone at the same time. This usually happens with individuals who are close to one another. My mother and I were very close. We referred to ourselves as twins. It was not uncommon for the both of us to have had the same dream the same night while living five hundred miles apart. The dreams were not similar, they were identical. How this happens, I do not know.

While working on my manuscript for this book, I was especially tired one day from working on it for so many long hours. I had become frustrated because I wasn't sure that what I had written that day was what I intended to say. Exhausted, I crawled into bed early. That evening I had a dream. My deceased husband was watching me in the distance and I noticed that he was smiling at me. It was as if I had climbed above the earth's eternal snowline to hear what I can only describe as "heavenly music" or like sounds of pure and endless Light. The music was always evolving into new sounds unlike anything ever heard on the earth plane. Imagine music being heard for the first time by a deaf person, or a blind person seeing. That would describe my joy upon hearing this beautiful celestial unearthly music.

There have been reports of some near-death experiencers hearing such heavenly music while on the other side. Descriptions of the music they heard was consistent with being not of this world. As I listened to the beautiful music, I felt such joy as if my very soul had entered a sacred domain where thousands of angels were singing to me.

Then, falling away like a speck in space, my dream ended with a gentle sound of stillness.

When I awoke the next morning, my heart was aflame with gratitude for my Beloved who brought me such a beautiful gift. There was no speculation that perhaps this was just a lovely dream. No, I know the difference after having prophetic message dreams my entire life. I'd like to believe that my Beloved brought that heavenly music to my ears so that I would know in my heart that this angelic music was a gift, a reward of sorts to encourage me to continue writing. He orchestrated a choir of angels to sing to me and to encourage me, AND he brought my husband along for the ride!

I have had numerous after-death communication experiences from deceased persons and each time, a sense of gratitude overcomes me knowing I was able to bring a message to someone from their loved one. During my waking consciousness, I feel I do not have the ability to receive those messages for whatever reason. But when I sleep, I am more "awake" to become a receiver of supernatural gifts that are veritable.

CHAPTER 13

INTEGRITY AS A CHOICE

For many years now, researchers have been studying the NDE phenomenon with the hope of proving, or at least suggesting, that life is a continuum. We have had over forty-plus years of investigation in this field. Thousands of near-death experiencers have been interviewed by reputable researchers, and science has now accepted as a scientific fact, that near-death experiences are real. They are not hallucinations, wishful thinking, and they are not pathological.

Common elements in these experiences include:
- Lifting out of one's physical body (OBE)
- Movement through a dark tunnel
- Meeting deceased loved ones or spiritual guides
- Life review
- Time or space is absent
- Seeing a light or presence with a feeling of warmth, love, and acceptance
- Feeling of not wanting to return
- Experiencing realms of great beauty; celestial music
- Gaining knowledge
- Loss of the fear of death

It is not surprising that much investigation and research has been devoted to this subject. We are very eager to learn as much as possible about the afterlife. Will we be reunited with our loved ones? What will we see and hear? The media is like a shark wanting to report the stories of near-death experiencers who had the most dramatic experiences for their media ratings. The experiencers themselves, write books, go on speaking tours to tell their beautiful stories. As a society, we are greatly comforted to learn what transpired during those in between moments of life and death. Society has been blessed to hear these reports from those willing to talk about their experiences.

For the experiencers themselves, their lives have been transformed for the most part into more loving, and compassionate individuals. Some change careers in order that they may help others. A middle-age secretary may go to school to become a nurse, or a business man may give up his corporate job to oversee a homeless shelter.

A powerful transformation took place in the life of art professor Howard Storm, who, after his encounter with Jesus during his NDE, abandoned his atheism and became a Christian minister. The literature is filled with accounts of near-death experiencers who rightfully claim, their lives were changed as a result of their mystical near-death experience.

However, not all near-death experiencers report a personal life transformation and it should not be assumed that all do. One woman confessed to me, *"Just because a person has a near-death experience, it doesn't mean they were changed in any way. Look at me, I'm still the same judgmental, unloving, and unforgiving person I always was."* I honor her truthfulness!

I have been in the near-death experience field for over

thirty-eight years. I have talked to many experiencers; I have studied them as well. What I have personally seen in some instances and in the near-death experience research literature, judging others, cynicism and unloving behavior seems not to be rare episodes of those who have had a near-death experience. We are being told by those reporting near-death experiences that such individuals return from their experiences, almost saint-like. That is not the case. The majority of near-death experiencers are speaking honestly and coming forth to tell us what happened to them. We don't have to assume that all experiencers are frauds. But some are.

I thought long and hard whether or not I should speak up about this subject. In the end, I decided to bring this matter to the public's attention. When I became aware of some near-death experiencers who wrote books who either lied or embellished their stories my heart cried for the innocent people that were being duped by them. For whatever reason, those individuals perhaps wanted to sell books or gain notoriety. Perhaps some people who had experiences that weren't very elaborate, simply wanted to feel their experiences merited the same kind of validation as others who had deeper experiences so they embellished them. Whatever one's reason for fabricating or embellishing their stories, I was heartbroken that someone could dishonor the One who loves us so unconditionally, and who wants us to be the best expression of our Divine Self as possible.

Leo Buscaglia said, *"Your talent is God's gift to you. What you do with it is your gift back to God."*

I think that's the reason I feel such an ache in my heart when someone lies or embellishes the gift they were given. I ask myself, *"How can they do this to God?"* That's right. What I do to self and others, I also do to God for we are the very presence of God within us. We are called to be truthful, but some dishonor the gift we have been given, and my heart cries.

Near-death and other spiritually transformative experiences were given to us by an act of grace. Most near-death experiencers will say their experiences were sacred and cherished experiences and would never think of fabricating or embellishing their stories. Our lives have been transformed in ways that *honor* the gift of grace we have been given. But in every profession, there are some bad apples in the bunch, and this NDE field is no different.

There is the case of Kevin and son Alex Malarkey. Kevin went to school and played football with my son, and afterwards Kevin became a Christian counselor. One day while driving his car, Kevin got distracted with his cell phone and was in a terrible auto accident. He was thrown from the car; his six-year-old son Alex, was severely injured and spent two months in a coma, only to awaken as a quadriplegic.

Kevin wrote the New York Times bestselling book, *The Boy Who Came Back from Heaven*. It was made into a TV movie and Kevin built a speaking career on it, traveling and giving interviews – alone. The only problem, the story of Alex dying and going to Heaven was made up. Alex said he made up the story because he wanted to get attention. On Alex's Facebook page, he posted: "One of the most deceptive books ever."

Apparently, Kevin Malarkey suppressed the truth for years until finally, he was exposed. The publisher, Tyndale, confirmed Alex's retraction with his father Kevin, and immediately took the book out of print and ordered all bookstores to take the books off the shelves. Why Amazon still sells the book that the author had admitted is a lie is beyond me. Amazon should pull it from their shelves just like many bookstores did. But I'm sure the reason it remains on Amazon is that as long as it sells, it brings in money.

Another incident a few years ago, involved a woman claiming to have had a near-death experience. National IANDS (International Association for Near-Death Studies, Inc.) is a world-wide reputable organization devoted to the research, education, and support of near-death experiences. It publishes a peer-reviewed scientific journal, sponsors yearly national conventions with leading researchers and spokespersons in the NDE community. Local chapters have been formed throughout the world.

National IANDS contacted all local group coordinators asking us to invite that woman who claimed to have had a near-death experience to speak to our IANDS groups, provide for her travel expenses and honorarium. The woman received many invitations to speak around the country until it was learned she did not have a near-death experience at all. National IANDS immediately contacted all local group coordinators alerting us of the fraud and requested that we no longer extend invitations for this woman to speak to our groups. A few years later, this woman publically apologized for the fraud and asked for forgiveness.

I have also personally known several individuals who embellished their experiences who continue to write books and speak about their experiences.

This will probably be an ongoing problem as long as there are certain individuals who want self-gain at the expense of being truthful and living from the purity of the spiritual center of their lives. How can we know whose stories are truthful and whose are deceptive? We won't unless they are exposed.

The most reliable and credible near-death experience accounts are those that were reported prior to the publication of Raymond Moody's book, *Life After Life* in 1976. In those cases, the individuals didn't have the exposure to the literature, television or other media outlets which reported this phenomena. They didn't have the opportunity to learn what others were reporting so that they could tell their stories in a similar manner. They spoke their truth as it was, and yet, their accounts were very similar to one another. That was the reason why Dr. Moody did his research to begin with. He kept hearing people describing a similar experience which happened to them when they died, and he understood that this was something that needed to be looked into. His research and book began the whirlwind research and public exposure to near-death experiences bringing comfort to many people interested in what happens after we die.

We live in a world where we are caught in the vices of ego and greed. We are being fed endless desires, manipulated by advertising and the media. We forget however, that life is sacred, reminding us that life is not about economic prosperity or getting more stuff, or duping others for our own self-centeredness. It's about honesty, truthfulness, emerging from the great mystery that is always present within, appearing to us as love and never doing harm to anyone in word or deed.

The literature is filled with research findings that imply that near-death experiencers return from their mystical-like experiences offering more love to self and others, are less judgmental, less materialistic, are more compassionate, and feel more spiritual, in addition to other blessings. Again, I reiterate, most are, but not all are. World noted NDE researchers P.M.H. Atwater and Kenneth Ring, PhD, have both reported this problem in their NDE research work and in their books as well.

It is fair to say that among *some* near-death experiencers, there are persons who are not all they seem to be. When I first came back from my own near-death experience in the early 1960's, and subsequent near-death-like or unitive experience in 1979, I thought everyone who had a near-death experience was Light-filled and would never harm another person in any way. I learned however, that wasn't the case. Several of my near-death experience acquaintances acted like Jekyll and Hyde in certain situations. On one hand they professed a loving persona to some and to others including myself, a rather vicious nature.

This malicious behavior also happened to a dear friend of mine, P.M.H. Atwater, noted near-death experience researcher who wrote in her book, *"Beyond the Light: What Isn't Being Said About Near-Death Experiences"* that her reputation as a researcher was slandered by a near-death experiencer who was intent upon destroying Atwater's investigative credibility. She talks about this crisis in her book.

I am an empath, able to experience another person's emotions. I'm not talking about normal empathy or compassion. An empath is able to feel as if he/she is *actually* experiencing what the other person is feeling. I hurt deeply in my core when someone is hurt by someone else, especially those near-death experiencers who profess to be so loving, yet act in unloving ways. It is hard for me to understand this.

Atwater's near-death experience research work focused on the aftereffects that people report after having had a near-death experience. After interviewing thousands of experiencers, she found that *"near-death survivors do not lose their individuality just because they have expanded into a more universal type of awareness."* Atwater writes, *"If anything, each of their given traits becomes more pronounced. Whatever existed before, becomes more noticeable after. This means weaknesses as well as strengths. Because of this experiencers can be difficult to deal with.* This was helpful for me to realize about others who did not express what I considered to be behaviors synonymous with the wisdom and love of the Light.

Atwater also explains in her book, *Beyond the Light,* many issues from childhood that are suppressed or ignored, surfaces following a near-death experience and that can interfere with the problems that many near-death experiencers appear to have. She writes, *"It's almost as if, in order to facilitate healing in others, one must first heal him-or-her."*

What makes one person become very loving afterwards and another not so? Perhaps the reason is to be found in the depth of one's experience or in their inability to fully integrate their experience into their personal life. Those who truly had deep mystical near-death experiences or other spiritually transformative experiences show an attribute of sensitivity to others first, setting aside self; always seeking the good of others. This selfless service is never rude or unkind. It is love transformed by a Higher Power indwelling, and they are aware of this love. If our need for love is met, we feel nourished in the depth of our being and there will be no need to be untrue to ourselves or to others.

What is going on within someone will define what they judge and what they don't judge. This could also be something they have repressed or are therefore unaware. Some near-death experiencers for instance, had early childhood experiences of abuse, strict social conditioning, religion, or something that taught them to accept some things and to reject others. This creates inner conflict and when the mind has lost touch with those feelings, emotions, needs and wants, the body can then end up being projected externally and being the cause of one's judgment, and thus, they become unaware of what the real problem may be.

Earl Nightingale said, *"When you judge others, you do not define them, you define yourself."*

In my opinion, judging others is a call for help, a call to love self. When a person doesn't like themselves, they feel the need to be negative about someone else in order to feel better about themselves. While some near-death experiencers may have experienced the profound love when on the other side of the veil, some can return from that love holding onto their ego needs of not loving self and projecting that onto others.

This is my plea to all who are tempted to write or speak untruths about their spiritual experiences, or who may treat others in hurtful ways; please think twice and don't do it. Integrity embodies the sum total of our being and actions. It isn't something we have; it's the essential nature of a human being. Who we are at the core of our being, the inherent perfection inside us all is the gift we have been born into. When we betray our inherent perfection inside us all, we betray the gift and the One we have been born into.

When we betray our inherent perfection by actions of dishonesty, deception, and unkindness, those actions mar the reflection of the immaculate Light that shines within us. *Our job is to offer as clean and clear a reflection as we possibly can so our hearts can become aware of the presence of God, shining in us and through us.* How do we do that?

St. Augustine said,

"Love, then do what you please."

One must also remember that when we die, we will have our life reviews. The majority of individuals who have returned from the other side who have been shown their life reviews, tell us that every single moment of our earthly lives are shown to us. The central message of life reviews are to show us the effects of one's actions on another and to ourselves.

One near-death experiencer said, *"Watching and re-experiencing all those events in my life changed everything. It was an opportunity to see and feel all the love I had shared, and more importantly, all the pain I caused. I was able to simultaneously re-experience not only my own feelings and thoughts, but those of all the other people I had ever interacted with. Seeing myself through their eyes was a humbling experience."*

From Raymond Moody's book, *The Light Beyond*: one experiencer said, *"When I die I am going to have to witness every single action of mine again, only this time actually feeling the effects I've had on others."*

I would suggest that any near-death experiencer who thinks about hurting another in word or deed, should remember that we will all have a life review at the end of our life. This earthly life is our opportunity to return to what is essential and true about ourselves, our Divine value. When we know and live from our Divine value, it helps others to know theirs. The near-death experience and all other spiritually transformative experiences are powerful awakening experiences that call us to action expressing the One Divine Power expressing through our beings on the human level.

Near-death experiencers and others who have had a mystical experience are discovering the gifts of their spiritual awakening. What's important now, after we have "seen the light," is to live the truth of our inner radiance while in earthly bodies. This is the first step on the inner path towards ever higher levels of reality, ever closer identification with our Source.

Help others as you have been helped, for you have been

guided and directed to know the Truth. Bless you, for as you grow strong in using the positive power of Spirit, you cannot use this power to harm anyone. No matter what your circumstances or the thoughts of people around you, continue to live in the kingdom of heaven where love is the only reality that brings us peace. Take each challenge as it comes and allow Spirit to work through you, and all will be well.

When we make the effort to discern God's mysterious Presence within by making the effort to love self and others, we won't desire to do those things that ultimately hurt ourselves. No matter how small it may seem, each personal shift in self-awareness and act of focus on the good and the positive, helps to bring the transformation of the entire planet. But first it must begin within each individual to cause this shift in the right direction.

If we are honest with ourselves and others, we are blessed with deep peace that we can only get when our soul has recognized who we actually are. Each lie, each deception, each act of dishonesty, and aggression, combines to create a bully that can destroy one's character.

Atwater cautions, *"Just because someone thinks he or she is spiritual doesn't mean that person is. Always look to the results, the consequences, because after effects cannot be faked."*

When everything is stripped away, our name, reputation, and character are all that remain. Integrity is the heart of character. Don't lose it. We all have our own opinions about everything and we all won't agree with everyone and that's okay. But the old familiar bottom line is: *"If you can't say something nice, well, you know the rest."*

CHAPTER 14

THE CALL TO BRING
HEAVEN INTO OUR WORLD

Our spiritual journey is an *inner journey*. We are seeking something found inside our own hearts which begins with an intentional longing for God and to discern God's call to us. This may come as a surprise, but the longing we sense is a gift given to us as God's longing for us. Deep within our being, our soul is trying to get our attention to listen to its' call. Love and silence are the keys to open the hidden places of the heart and from where the most glorious intimacy with the mystery beyond our mental or physical grasp can be found.

We are all Light-beings of consciousness that each of us reflects the Sacred when we are in touch with the Sacred at every step of our spiritual journey. Each step we take along the path allows us to become more aware that a process is involved, that the process is within us and outside us. The point of it all is to let ourselves become so aware of the hidden treasure within us that will render us with great truth and inspiration. It takes work to cultivate these higher gifts and if we do not develop our awareness to this greater reality, we are like a man who owns a gold mine, but does not know its value and starves to death for want of food.

Strange as it may seem, hardship has a part to play in all true revelation. If we had no desire for betterment there would be no incentive to reach beyond our limited perception of ourselves and the circumstances that we face in our daily lives. Were it not for the rigor of winter, would we not appreciate the change that comes in bringing spring into bloom?

The progress of our world is largely dependent upon the Light-workers, you and I, who are working with Divine Intent, breaking down old barriers, and conveying ideals larger than ourselves. I am not indulging in a wild flight of imagination my friends. Our real and gifted selves are flashing with Spirit, if only we will get out of our ego's way and reveal what we are capable of creating. Our dreams and ideals are larger than ourselves; our aspirations have made it possible for us to tap into a greater Source than that of knowledge, the Source of Wisdom Itself.

It is a great responsibility to be gifted with the powers of the soul that for many, lie dormant. The world has need of the Light, of the powers of every soul. Our little Lights fused together may shed a great radiance whereby the lesser ones can merge with our little Lights together bringing law and order into a finer civilization than the world has yet seen.

The essence of life is Spirit, a priceless revelation of a power which is indefinable in itself, but which can be revealed through one's Higher Self capable of voicing its reality. Mind is like a plant growing, expanding, and it needs nourishment of the right sort. It needs sunshine and real joy to flourish. Choose with care the path you seek to follow, and use it with purpose, so that one of the greatest gifts with which you are endowed shall become a real blessing for you, drawing you upward. Trust your soul to bring you Light **if you really desire to find it.**

Let's face it. Humanity still has a long way to go before we all reach that state of non-ego where we will then be able to bring Heaven down to earth, or earth up to Heaven. Until then, we must learn all we can about our spiritual nature while we are inhabiting these physical bodies so that humanity can evolve toward the higher consciousness that awaits us.

We frequently hear people say that if God had intended us to be so spiritually endowed with the powers of the Spirit, He would have given them to us already developed. All life develops from an embryo. We don't have fully developed spiritual powers already manifested, but they do exist in embryo in every human being. If humanity is ever to reach greater perfection, the means by which progress is to be accomplished must be latent in each and every human being, awaiting its birth.

There are, however, degrees of awareness. Some people's soul wisdom is very near the surface, while others may have to develop it for years before their higher perceptions begin to come to life. God has given us the innate tools to develop our soul and to use our life force for good. When we have developed an inwardly sound personality through whom the Divine Presence within can flow, then we have made real progress. Then when the hard knocks come, as they are bound to come, the soul of the individual has created for itself such a strong foundation that it remains strong. We can depend on the same Power that created the universe. Why would we want to rely on ourselves? Head knowledge helps us understand, but only a humble heart can help us live a Divine life. Such joy we receive when we know that God is doing the work of our transformation – minute by minute.

Rumi wrote:

"Knock and He'll open the door.
Vanish and He'll make you shine like the sun.
Fall, and He'll raise you to the Heavens.
Become nothing, and He'll turn you into everything.

Yes, God works through us, and in helping each other we widen our understanding and increase our capacity for drawing upon Spirit for strength and enlightenment. Minute by minute, if we choose to remain ignorant because we will not employ the courage to stay on the path toward union with God, well, there is always another life, but we will first have to experience a life review after we die. We will then see how many missed opportunities we had to grow spiritually while inhabiting this earth school. As we attain the consciousness of our real Self, the Reality of our Divine Consciousness, we attain immortality. And that can be achieved here and now. It results in being *in* the world but not *of* it.

That moment by God's Grace I merged into Oneness with Him in 1979 changed my life forever. I have been blessed to move beyond belief into the knowingness that God is the Loving Intelligence behind all forces of creation. I understood then as I continue to know now, that God is Love, Living Love happening in each moment. He did not create us to suffer, which is a concept born of our choice to be separate, which is simply our ego messing with our minds insisting on doing things "our way." God never moves away from us; we move away from Him by focusing on ourselves, our problems, and our desires. Pretending we don't need help robs God of the opportunity to give us everything we need.

When we commit ourselves to the mystical path toward union with God, there will be changes not only in us, but in those around us as well. For as the Light pours from us, it paves the way for others to follow. Know that as we open ourselves to the Holy Spirit within, we will receive the consciousness which is attuned with our innermost Divine Teacher.

Moving forward is easy when we allow our Great Teacher to lead us along the mystical path. The growth of our spiritual awareness, our oneness with God and all, will open doors to our next step in growth, helping to drop our fears and move ahead. When we decide to do this, our choice will be honored. We will find we are protected, guided, loved and fed power to accomplish what we thought we couldn't do.

Life is a wonderful, long journey, filled with the joy of accomplishment, of giving and growing, of serving and loving. We are never alone, though at times we believe we are. If we can trust and walk forward in faith, we set in motion the power of Spirit within to make the wholeness which already exists come forth, and manifest in form.

The mystical path toward wholeness as I stated earlier, is a long and difficult journey. Along the way, we will be asked to heal ourselves from past injustices, and seeing all those wounds from the ego's eyes. The goal is to see through the soul's eyes where we are no longer living in the past, but living fully in the present. This doesn't mean that we forget what happened in the past. It does mean however, that we make a choice to no longer let the past dictate who we are in the present by continually rehashing the wounds that were once caused.

I had my share of wounds, having been violently raped twice during my lifetime. It took a while before coming to grips of what happened and the damage it would do to my spirit. But I made a choice to forgive the attackers in order to heal myself of that trauma. I made the choice to listen to my inner "voice" that guided me in making that decision, a decision that I am grateful I made. When we call upon our Spirit to help us change the way we look at things, Spirit will help heal us. Freeing ourselves from the energy of the ego to the energy of the soul makes all the difference.

Take a second to see how blessed you are. Stop and smell the roses – then stop a moment longer and marvel over the amazing process of their growth. You and I are marvels of God's creation as well. Our very soul originates from God and essentially possesses the same qualities as God, love, compassion, and wisdom. Our purpose is to discover our true nature – the exquisite diamond within us and to receive the Divine gifts we have been created to receive. God is always communicating with us, but those who cling to ego can't hear His Voice very well.

Intuitive knowledge is a gift that we have without a conscious action on our part. We often describe intuition as a gut feeling as coming from the heart. It is a God-given and innate knowledge and core component of our spiritual development. How many times we may have ignored our intuition, only to realize in retrospect that we should have listened to that still small voice within.

For a long time many people thought there was no such thing as human intuition. But now, there seems to be scientific documentation to suggest that it is very real. A study has been published in the peer-reviewed journal *Psychological Science*. Associate Professor Joel Pearson and his team of investigators at the University New South Wales, Australia conducted experiments with more than 100 students who were asked to report whether a series of black dots on a computer screen were moving left or right.

At the same time, and without their knowledge, the students were presented with emotional images that had been made invisible through continuous flash suppression. Some images were positive, like puppies and flowers; others were negative, such as a snake.

The students were unaware that their brains were processing this emotional information. But registering the combination of positive and negative images boosted their decision accuracy, making them faster and more confident in determining the direction of the moving dots.

Associate Professor Pearson said, *"Subjects were using unconscious emotional information as evidence to help them make a decision."* He claims that *"While it was widely accepted that people act intuitively or make intuitive decisions, no one's been able to show that unconscious, rapid emotions can actually affect our decisions. This is the first time it's been done."*

Pearson is very excited about the study, suggesting that "intuition improved over time, and that the mechanisms of intuition can be improved with practice." He also said, *"It could be used to train people to rely more on the emotional information in their brain and their body, rather than just logical, conscious information."*

What an amazing blessing. What an incredible and caring God we have to provide within us what we need to live an amazing life. He works in our life moment by moment, day by day; conforms us to His likeness; builds a relationship with us; comforts us in our hurts; and empowers us.

"Think...of the world you carry within you."
–Rainer Maria Rilke

CHAPTER 15
ENTER INTO COMMUNION WITH GOD

I have been known to say many times, *"Following my unitive experience, the Light/God never left me. I feel God's Loving Presence with me every day."* Often times the Presence overwhelms me and I fall on my knees bursting out with tears of joy. The Presence is so strong that all my silent thoughts would gush into tears like rain pouring into sunshine.

Every day is felt like a communion between self and my Beloved, praying and talking to Him most of the day. Or I just sit quietly in silence where I wait to feel the most incredible feelings of love, as if my inner being is lit up with His Presence. Honestly, I can say that this feeling is different from "believing" that God's Presence is being made known to me. It's a direct experiential "knowing" of His Presence within me, and it overwhelms me. I have learned to recognize this Sacred Presence and when I do, I set aside the ramblings of my mind and silently rest, sitting in wonder for as long as possible as my soul-self refreshes itself in union with God.

Resting from words that want to clutter my mind, I let them drop from my head to my heart. It takes great patience and time to discover that deep listening place, but I let my Beloved know I'm here, waiting and anticipating Him. In this spirit, I can almost hear my internal wisdom speaking to me; *"Nancy, let go and let God. It will all unfold as it unfolds."* It is within that deep place where I can observe the moment, the holiness of it and trust it.

When I reach my "center" and remain in the stillness of who I am, who I've become, I hold my heart with gentleness and kindness, enfolding it with a blanket of love and a feeling of nothingness.

Other times I can be looking out the window and I begin talking to God. Pretty soon, I am giving a discourse on some spiritual message that I assume God inspired me with. It's as if I am standing before an imaginary audience and preaching God's message of love. Is that odd? It's just that I get so filled up with His Spirit that I can't keep it inside of me so I talk to some imaginary audience, even if that audience is composed only of squirrels and birds. Those talks seem to bubble up from the Source of inner consciousness unintentionally, pressing on my soul like a pent-up storm craving for outlet. Age has crept upon me and I am no longer able to travel to give talks. So these days, my only audience is my Beloved and when He calls me to write more books.

Most of the times those talks are pretty darn beautiful if I must say so. But I can't remember what I said after I finish my talk. Once I tried to have a tape recorder playing, but my ego got in the way and I wasn't able to speak with the beauty and clarity as I always did. I do believe those "talks" are God inspired when my ego isn't clamoring for my attention when I start talking to God. The communion is deep. Something beautiful overtakes me, filling me up with the Spirit of the Beloved. Am I crazy? No. To me, this is normal Divine Love being spilled out of me beyond my control. But once ego looms its egotistical voice, I'm back to ordinary consciousness and wondering what I will make for dinner or planning what my next activity will be.

My love for the Sacred One is deeper than the deep sea and wider than the whole of the universe.

"Extinguish my eyes, I'll go on seeing you.
Seal my ears, I'll go on hearing you.
And without feet I can make my way to you,
Without a mouth I can swear your name.
Break off my arms, I'll take hold of you
With my heart as with a hand.
Stop my heart, and my brain will start to beat.
And if I consume my brain with fire,
I'll feel you burn in every drop of my blood.
                                        –Rainer Maria Rilke

In studying the mystics and saints for this book, many times I felt so moved by their words that a single tear would glisten in the corner of my eye. I understood those words as if they were holding my hand and letting me experience the rapture of their own hearts as they put their love for our Beloved into words. Those words jumped off the pages of their writings and into my heart where they settled into a blissful feeling as if God Himself were speaking to me. (And He probably was!) I hope that when you read the mystics and the Saints words, they may ignite within you, an inner voice that will take you as well to that hidden place of Divine Love within.

"The wonderful effect of Divine Love: Nothing is sweeter than love, nothing stronger, nothing higher, nothing broader; nothing is more lovely, nothing richer, and nothing better in heaven or on earth. Love is born of God and it cannot rest anywhere but in God, beyond all created things."

–Thomas `a kempis

Flemish mystic John of Ruysbroeck said:

"These two spirits – that is, our spirit and the Spirit of God – cast a radiant light upon one another and each reveals to the other its countenance. This makes the two spirits incessantly strive after one another in love. Each demands of the other what it is, and each offers to the other and invites it to accept what it is. This makes these loving spirits lose themselves in one another. God's touch and his giving of himself, together with our striving in love and our giving of ourselves in return – this is what sets love on a firm foundation."

I receive many emails from people from all parts of the world who read my books and who felt they needed to tell me how their lives were changed after reading my books. I am quick to point out to them that I didn't change their lives, it was the *Holy Spirit in them* who changed their lives whose voice within allowed them to open their minds and hearts to the gift of grace they received from their Divine Source. I can't accept any credit for that. All glory be to God who changed that person's heart!

Some people had very bad life experiences and felt God no longer loved them. They felt they could not initiate a relationship with God for fear that God would punish them for the way they lived their lives. But when they read how I was treated by a priest who had convinced me I was the scum of the earth and God no longer loved me, they could identify with the pain and sorrow I felt. They went through something similar and felt rotten to the core as well. My healing took place during my unitive experience, and their healing came about after reading my books. God will use any means of bringing His Love to us to heal our brokenness. A book, a conversation, synchronicity, a spiritual experience, prayer, an open heart. His Love for us longs to comfort us and return us to our rightful birthright of loving union with Him.

> *"You have to keep breaking your heart until it OPENS."*
> —Rumi

I have always known from my lessons from my Great Teacher, that everything that happens to us is an opportunity for our spiritual growth or for someone else's growth. I went through sixteen years of being brainwashed by a priest who believed he was doing his job as a Christian counselor. I never felt angry toward him or toward God for what happened to me. I was able to look back at that part of my life to see how such a bad experience could be used for good later on in my life. I have been able to help so many people who have been in my shoes and who were not able to see themselves as good people. I became their beacon of hope that God loves them just the way they are. God uses me in that way, and I am so grateful. I often tell folks who are hurting like that what Saint Augustine said:

"God loves each of us as if there were only one of us."

Let that quote sink in folks. We're talking about how God loves us unconditionally, no strings attached. Here are some of my favorite quotes to bring home this message for you....

"We please Him most not by frantically trying to make ourselves good but by throwing ourselves into His arms with all our imperfections, and believing that He understands everything and loves us still."

–A. W. Tozer

"Our faults are like a grain of sand beside the great mountain of the mercies of God."

–Saint Jean Baptiste Marie Vianney

"God does not wish us to remember what He is willing to forget"

–George Arthur Buttrick

"Trust the past to the mercy of God, the present to His Love, and the future to His providence.

–Saint Augustine

Entering into communion with God is so simple and oh so beautiful! Our souls are transparent to God like a shining sun, so nothing can be hidden from our Beloved. We do not need to approach our Beloved from fear, but from love. We are a child of the One who loves us beyond words and He wants us to draw near to Him. Drawing our attention away from our daily chaos and entering the state of prayer is a way of seeking the peace of the Divine Presence within us. God doesn't require that we approach Him with a special way of prayer; we just have to talk to Him. It's easy.

"Whether we realize it or not, a prayer is the encounter of God's thirst with ours. God thirsts that we may thirst for Him.

–Saint Augustine

"Prayer enlarges the heart until it is capable of containing God's gift of Himself.

–Mother Theresa

"Prayer is the song of the heart. It reaches the ear of God even if it is mingled with the cry and tumult of a thousand men.

–Kahlil Gibran

"A man prayed, and at first he thought that prayer was talking. But he became more and more quiet until in the end he realized that prayer is listening."

–Soren Kierkegaard

Appreciating each moment that draws us closer to our Beloved is a blessing indeed. This book I am writing can be summed up in these few words. The degree in which one opens one's consciousness to the inflow of the Presence or loving awareness of God, in that degree will one demonstrate that reality of being in one's outer reality.

I consider waking up in the morning with the conscious awareness that when my eyes open, I am aware of my Beloved's Presence with me. Once that awareness has been made, then for the rest of my day all I have to do is look over my shoulder and watch God at work.

There is always a sense of gratitude that oozes from me every day acknowledging that on my own human effort, I can do nothing. I know with absolute conviction that my Beloved and I are doing everything together, team-mates in the course of daily life.

Jesus said, *"I can of mine own self do nothing."* John 5:30 and in Galatians 2:20, Paul said, *"I live; yet not I, but Christ liveth in me."*

Every bit of good that we do is the Divine Presence within acting through us. Shouldn't that inspire us to feel gratitude to the One who is always going before us, who comes up behind us, and walks beside us? Even though there is such a Presence, there must be a conscious realization of that Presence.

We are by nature, hurried individuals who are uncomfortable not being able to see around the bend. There are times not at the beginning nor the end of the journey but the mid-points when we feel uncomfortable and lack the control to manifest the results we desire. And yet, we are called to enter into the Mystery of God and sharing in the Sacred place called time. Here we can have the faith that God's Hand is leading the way. Teilhard de Chardin wrote a beautiful poem about waiting upon our Beloved when we are anxious to see results.

Patient Trust

Above all, trust in the slow work of God.
We are quite naturally impatient in everything
To reach the end without delay.
We should like to skip the intermediate stages.
We are impatient of being on the way to something
Unknown, something new.
And yet it is the law of all progress
That it is made by passing through
Some stages of instability
And that it may take a very long time.

And so I think it is with you;
Your ideas mature gradually - let them grow,
Let them shape themselves, without undue haste.
Don't try to force them on,
As though you could be today what time
(that is to say, grace and circumstances acting on your
own good will)
Will make of you tomorrow.

Only God could say what this new spirit
Gradually forming within you will be.
Give our Lord the benefit of believing
That His hand is leading you,
And accept the anxiety of feeling yourself
In suspense and incomplete.

CHAPTER 16
LOVE IS THE KEY

The mystic path is always a demanding challenge to let the Spirit completely remake us according to the beautiful demands of love. God's love for us is unconditional, no strings attached. Many near-death experiencers and others who have had mystical spiritually transformative experiences have received this gift of God's grace, knowing that unconditional love is different from the conditional love we all know. If you are nice to me, I'll be nice to you and so on. That's conditional love. In mystical experience, we know unconditional love directly and it changes our lives.

Recall in an earlier chapter that my Great Teacher said to me, *"Love is the key to the universe; you must all learn to live in peace and harmony with one another while you have the chance."* I understood that we are here participating in various classrooms in this earth school to learn our lessons of unconditional love before our physical bodies return to dust.

> *"We come from Love; we are sustained in Love, and to Love we shall return."*
>
> –Christian saying

Within us is the Holy Presence of God. In that innermost center of ourselves, our awareness of that Sacredness is hidden unless we are made aware through prayer, meditation, faith, and contemplation. When discovered, it is the most profound relationship we can have and will ever have. My understanding while merged into oneness with God during my unitive experience, is that it is God's will for us that we become totally transformed into love itself, like Him.

In all my readings of the mystics and saints, they always spoke of some kind of inner purification that is necessary in order to arrive at a deeper union with God. During one part of my unitive experience, I was shown an onion and all its layers which symbolically depicted the negative aspects of ourselves which hide the core of our being, our soul. I understood that we are supposed to remove each layer of that onion, each false layer of ourselves in order that we may reveal that sweetest core of the onion, or the sweetest core of our essence, the soul. We have built so many layers of negative factors to hide our essence like guilt, hatred, jealousy, fear, etc. Removing each layer of our false self purifies our inner self so that the essence of our true self can be revealed.

The very breath of the inner life is love and the very essence of life. We exist because of love. Love is not learned, it is felt; it is carried within, like an elevator that can take you down into the depths, beneath the surface of the mind. It is the essential resource in the individual's spiritual transformation leading to the development of a higher spiritual vibration. Pure Divine love is the highest possible vibration, and it is this love that we are learning to awaken to while in earth school.

Love that is understood by man is not the Divine love I am speaking about. Many people are living their lives walking around in a lower-vibrational pathway of fear, feigning their love, and confusing it with a selfish need to display their love for others because of guilt, feelings of obligation, or worries that others won't like us or will leave us if we don't help them.

True love doesn't involve thinking about what we'll receive. The act of giving from love is so joyful that it is its own reward. Cultivating a good heart of compassion, and small acts of kindness and love is a good way of honoring our loving true self, and is always Divinely guided by an intuitive thought or feeling to help someone without expecting anything in return.

"Lord, grant that I might not so much seek to be loved as to love."

—Saint Francis of Assisi

The God who revealed Himself to me during my unitive experience was **pure love** who had no judgment, fear, anger, or any negativity whatsoever. The **totality** of God's Being was pure, unconditional love which means that there was no part of God that was less than pure love. It was impossible for even a smidgeon of negative energy to be part of God's unflawed Being.

I was shown how perfect and pure His love was for me and for **everyone** as well. We were created *from* God and *by* God, including everything in the universe. Everything includes the tiniest quarks and atoms to the far reaches of the multi-universes. There is no part of us that is separate or away from our Beloved. Think of that for a moment and let that profound truth sink in. *You* are inside of God, along with every other person, and everything you can see, smell, touch, hear, and taste! We live within the love of God right now. We are continually being bathed in the highest vibration of pure Divine love, and seen as we really are: a brilliant being of pure Divine love.

Our true self, or soul knows this truth about ourselves, but we humans forgot that this pure love is our true identity. Instead of living and expressing ourselves from our true selves of pure love, we take action from a place of fear, helplessness and powerlessness which is generated from a lower-vibrational choice.

Our earth school classroom will provide us with ample opportunities to return and keep us centered in our true self if we choose to learn the lessons. Should we decide to study and follow love's direction, we will begin to hear things and see things that we did not hear and see before. We will have greater vision and more understanding, realizing love's validity and its great relevance to the world we have to face. Our hands become the hands of God when we allow Him to love others through us.

"Love alone is capable of uniting beings in such a way as to complete and fulfill them, for it alone takes them and joins them by what is deepest in themselves."
    –Pierre Teilhard de Chardin

"Don't shine so others can see you. Shine so that through you others can see Him"
    –C. S. Lewis

Pure Divine love comes from our Source- the greatest love of our lives, the Source of our purpose for being in the world. We can't give this Sacred love to ourselves. It must come as a gift revealed to us from a greater Source that lives beyond the realm of the intellect. It simply requires that we respond when this Divine love knocks upon the door of our consciousness. It asks us to put aside our prejudices, anger, or our resentments.

"Your task is not to seek for love, but merely to seek and find all the barriers within yourself that you have built against it."

–Rumi

Should you become aware of this pure unconditional love, then you must share it with others. God's gift of Divine love is a gift to the world, but so many people are unaware that this gift lies dormant within their interior self. Why this gift isn't automatically recognized is, perhaps God doesn't want to force anything on us that we don't actually desire or choose for ourselves. Those of us who are aware of this gift must bear witness and prepare humanity for a future that will be representative of Divine Will and Purpose.

"Love is our true destiny. We do not find the meaning of life by ourselves alone – we find it together."

–Thomas Merton

We are all a part of the unfolding of life, rather than apart from it. How would your life change if you made every decision based on true love? I would like to suggest that there will be times when you aren't so hard on yourself, times when you find old behaviors and ways of thinking have dropped away. Your heart goes out to those who are hurting. You pay more attention to being kind in what you say and do.

The mystics and the saints tell us that the interior life must be more important to us than the ego's distractions we often focus on. To the one who loves well, one's mind is opened, and one is then able to see the beauty within self, first, and then within others. In giving to another, we give to ourselves. The pleasure is not so much in receiving as in giving. Know that it is God within you Who is giving, Who is sharing His Light, spreading His joy and His love to all His children, through you.

> *"The Lord doesn't look so much at the greatness of our works, as at the love with which they are done. Thus, even though our works are small, they will have the value our love for Him would have merited had they been great."*
> –Saint Teresa of Avila

When I read what St. Teresa wrote, I was reminded of something my Great Teacher taught me during my unitive experience. The Light explained to me that the smallest expression of a loving kindness was just as momentous as the greatest loving kindness. For a moment I didn't understand because my ego-self had always believed many actions to be either large or small, you know, in a linear way. For instance, if I become a New York Times best-selling author, then I will have pleased God to the best of my ability. If only a handful of people read my book, then I haven't done great work for God. So is the ego's voice.

My Great Teacher taught me that He isn't very interested in our material success in the world. He is more interested in how much we love one another. Some people have big hearts and they find it easy to love others, while some find it harder to love others. What matters to God is no matter how great or how small our ability to love others may be, God is extremely pleased with whatever measure of love we are able to give.

During my unitive experience, my Beloved revealed to me that anytime one acts from a loving manner to perform a simple act of kindness, the person is drawing from one's inner presence of Divine love. God is love, therefore, simple acts of kindness or works are those instances when from our inner temple, we "let God out" and bless someone. Love is love. There is no rating scale where God's love is concerned. All will be blessed equally whenever a loving act or kindness is being expressed because love is the greatest power in the source of creation. Tapping into it whenever we have the opportunity to share it with someone is like a world of sunshine breaking through the dark night.

"You know well enough that our Lord does not look so much at the greatness of our actions nor even at their difficulty, but at the love with which we do them."

–Saint Therese of Lisieux

FINDING GOD IN ALL THINGS

Saint Ignatius Loyola, founder of the Jesuits, established the Society of Jesus in 1540. He instructed those early Jesuits to go out and "find God in all things." This was a way of discerning God's presence in everyday lives.

"God is not remote from us. He is at the point of my pen, my pick, my paintbrush, my needle – and my heart and my thoughts."

–Pierre Teilhard de Chardin

To be able to be aware of God in all places and things is a wonderful way of bringing the awareness that our Beloved is with us at all times. God is not somewhere far away up in the sky, distant from us, but nearer to us than our heartbeat. We only have to open our eyes and hearts to recognize His presence in many faces and places.

Here are some examples in my own life where I found God.

- I saw God in my friend who gave me some yellow roses to comfort me on the anniversary date of my husband's death.
- I saw God in the grocery cashier's smile who gave me a few minutes of her busy work time to wish me a good day.
- I saw God in the township worker walking alongside the ditch picking up the trash that people threw out of their car windows and onto my grass.
- I saw God in my friend's email message supporting me as I worked on my book manuscript.
- I saw God on Facebook in the children's smiling faces.
- I saw God in the nurse who held my hand while I went under anesthesia.
- I saw God in the truck driver who paused to allow me entry onto the busy road.
- I saw God in those people who rescued animals from abuse and gave them a forever home.
- I saw God in the sunrise and in the sunset.
- I saw God while walking through the woods; in the trees, in the wildflowers, and in the gentle stream flowing beside me.
- I saw God in the homeless woman panhandling on the sidewalk.

- I always see God in my sons' hearts when they offer me their help now that I am getting older and unable to do some things on my own.

Think about your own examples and how blessed you are to "see God in many faces and places."

"A billion stars go spinning through the night, glittering above your head. But in you is the presence that will be when all the stars are dead."
                                                    —Rainer Maria Rilke

Walk forward, dear one, into a new life; a life of joy, a life of peace, a life of grace, for God's grace is upon you. Watch yourself as you move forward along the mystical path for which you are called. Watch yourself grow with ease. Observe yourself love more than you have ever loved. Watch yourself communicate on a higher level, as you tune into your Divine nature and call forth the Divinity in all those around you. For as you know the nature of yourself and your grace, you know the Divine nature of every man, woman and child in the universe.

Love your true nature with all your heart, with all your soul, with all your mind, for your true nature is the Christ within you which is Divine; it is you.

"Faith is what gets you started. Hope is what keeps you going. Love is what brings you to the end."
                                                    —Mother Angelica, PCPA

I pray that you will stay on the mystical path toward ultimate union with God, whether God grants you that gift during this lifetime, or another.

> *"Divinity never forces itself upon you. If you are willing, it is always there for you. If you are not willing, it is not there for you. So all you need to do is create the right kind of willingness and receptivity. Just to bow down and not have a will of your own is the biggest receptivity. It is the easiest way to receive."*
>
> —Sadhguru

In closing, writing this book with my Beloved has been my gift to Him first and foremost, to keep my promise to write what He entrusted me with. It is my hope that I have inspired others to celebrate a reality one cannot see, but one that is available to experience. Allow these final words to become your motivation to keep you looking forward to a greater reality, filled with the wonder of discovery.

"Dear past, thank you for all the life lessons you have taught me. Dear future, I am ready now."

CHAPTER 17
SUMMARY

We began this book discussing what the unitive experience was and how by God's Grace, I was given that experience. We learned that many near-death and other spiritually transformative experiences are awakening experiences, not an end in themselves. We then went on to talk about mysticism, the saints, and developing the self toward a higher spiritual Self where love and compassion purges the ego's willful control over us. We talked about God's unconditional love for every one of us, with no exceptions, and how we are being asked as Meister Eckhart said:

> *"Become in all things a God seeker and a God finder, at all times and in all places."*

The greatest truth I can share with humanity is that we have within us, the very presence of God in what we call our soul. We were created from and in God so at the core of our being, we are pure Divine Spirit. To the degree we are able to realize this not from "head knowledge," but from "heart knowledge," will we be able to attain a new perspective toward reality *beyond* our everyday world, and relate to our outer reality from our original, unaltered true nature.

There are no guarantees that God will grant you His Grace of having a unitive experience. That gift cannot be brought about merely by one's own attempt to have such an experience. No matter how saintly a life one may lead, the unitive experience is granted by God and God alone. All I can do as someone who was granted that Sacred unitive experience is to point out the path that eventually leads there, a path of *deliberately* choosing to turn your attention within to the living God until it becomes habitual.

This state of continually turning within results in a continuous exchange of love between you and our Beloved. No longer do you need to seek for it by *outward* acts. In this state of continually being turned to God, you are abiding in the love of God. This inward attraction becomes more and more powerful, deep, inward, hidden and outwardly imperceptible.

I cannot coerce God to give anyone the experience of union with Him. However, all I can do is witness to that act of God to affirm that the unitive experience is a reality. It is the reality we return to after our earthly lives are through, but in rare instances, some individuals are granted that gift during earthly life. All I can do is help someone to recognize there is a path toward transformation in which one allows one's soul the consent to increase the soul's purity in exact proportion to the loss of self.

In this state of continually being turned to God, the soul is expressing itself as a continuous exchange of love between the soul and God. To the degree we minimize the personal ego and attain the consciousness of our real Self, the Divine Presence within, we attain unfathomed joys.

My own eyes like stars have seen unfathomed joys and

love unspeakable in both my inner and outer worlds. My desire is that all will one day see with the same eyes.

"We must close our eyes and invoke a new manner of seeing a wakefulness that is the birthright of us all, though few put it to use."

–Plotinus

This earthly life is precious. It is like a bubble blown up in the air, gently reaching its peak only to burst into oblivion. For that reason, we must remember that we are here in earth school to learn the lesson of unconditional love. We will be given many daily opportunities to learn that lesson. Pay attention!

The greatest love we can offer to someone is to transform our inner life so that others are attracted to one's genuine example of goodness. Love is not what the ego human mind *wants* it to be, but always what it *really* is.

Remember, we are here to develop our spiritual vibration by finding our true identity, bearing the fruits of love, understanding, and compassion so that we can enter a higher spiritual dimension in the afterlife.

"In my Father's house are many mansions."

–(John 14:2)

The work is to be done now! Don't procrastinate! There is a Hebrew saying, *if not now, when?*

"Take care of your body as if you were going to live forever;
And take care of your soul as if you were going to die tomorrow."

—Saint Augustine

LIFE'S TOO SHORT

Life's too short to wake up in the morning with regrets,
so.....
Love the people who treat you right.
Forget about the ones who don't.
Believe that everything happens for a reason.
If you get the chance, TAKE IT!
If it changed your life, LET IT!
Nobody said it would be easy.....
Just that it would be worth it!

—Unknown

ABOUT THE AUTHOR

Nancy Clark is an international award-winning author whose passion is to inspire others to comprehend the core message of near-death and other mystical spiritually transformative experiences. She has given talks around the country, been interviewed on radio and television, and has been a consultant to journalists. She is the founder and facilitator for the International Association for Near-Death Studies (IANDS) in Columbus, OH; member, Academy for Spiritual and Consciousness Studies; member, American Center for the Integration for Spiritually Transformative Experiences. Nancy is a graduate of Women's Medical College specializing in cytology (study of cells) and has taught cytology and conducted cytology cancer research at a major university.

Visit her at: www.freewebs.com/nancy-clark

The author wishes to thank you for reading this book. If you feel that others would benefit from reading it as well, then please write a review of this book on Amazon.com. This is the best way the book can reach others.

If you would like to contact Nancy Clark to share your thoughts, questions, or any feedback that you may have; feel free to email her at: nancyclarkauthor@gmail.com. Autographed books can be ordered directly from the author. Please email her for more information.

OTHER BOOKS BY NANCY CLARK

Hear His Voice: The Light's Message for Humanity

My Beloved: Messages From God's Heart to Your Heart

Stop Trying to Fix Me: I'm Grieving As Fast As I Can

Divine Moments: Ordinary People Having Spiritually Transformative Experiences

Gottliche Momente – (Published in Germany)

Revelations From the Light: What I Learned About Life's Purposes

HIGH PRAISE AND ENDORSEMENTS FOR NANCY CLARK'S BOOKS

Eben Alexander III, M.D., New York Times bestselling author

Larry Dossey, M.D., New York Times bestselling author

Bernie Siegel, M.D., New York Times bestselling author

Dannion Brinkley, New York Times bestselling author

Jeffrey Long, M.D., New York Times bestselling author

Howard Storm, New York Times bestselling author

William Guggenheim, Bestselling author

John W. White, International bestselling author

Rodney Charles, Bestselling author

Kenneth Ring, PhD, World renowned NDE researcher and author

P.M.H. Atwater, L.H.D, World renowned NDE researcher and author

Yolaine Stout, President ACISTE, American Center for the Integration of Spiritually Transformative Experiences

Jim Tressel, Former Ohio State University head football coach

Steven Fanning, PhD, Author; Associate professor of history, University of Illinois at Chicago

Jeff Olsen, Author

Vernon Sylvest, M.D., Author

Jody Long, JD, www.nderf.org

Evelyn Elsaesser-Valarino, Author

Pam Kircher, M.D.,Author

Mark Pitstick, MA, DC, Author; Eternea's Director of Education

Rev. John W. Price, Author

Jim Auer, journalist and Author

Claudia Carawan, Singer, Songwriter

Josie Varga, Author

David Sunfellow, Author

Rev. Joyce Fisher Pierce, VA

Rev. Juliet Nightingale, Radio Show Host

William Hoover, M.D.

Pat Stillisano, DDS

Mark Lutz, MA

Martha St. Claire, MA, Counselor, Educator

Randy Klinger, NDE conference organizer and artist

CPSIA information can be obtained
at www.ICGtesting.com
Printed in the USA
FSHW011958150219
55722FS